Simon Stephens

Motortown

D1347858

Published by Methuen Drama 2006

3 5 7 9 10 8 6 4 2

First published in 2006 by
Methuen Drama
A&C Black Publishers Ltd
36 Soho Square
London W1D 3QY

A CIP catalogue record for this book is available from
the British Library

ISBN: 978 0 413 77607 5

Typeset by Country Setting, Kingsdown, Kent

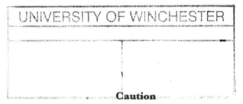

Caution

All rights in this play are strictly reserved. Application for
performance, etc. should be made before rehearsals begin to
Casarotto Ramsay & Associates Ltd, Waverley House,
7–12 Noel Street, London W1F 8GQ

No performance may be given unless a licence has been obtained

ROYAL COURT

Royal Court Theatre presents

MOTORTOWN
by **Simon Stephens**

First performance at the Royal Court Jerwood Theatre Downstairs,
Sloane Square, London on 21st April 2006.

Supported by JERWOOD NEW PLAYWRIGHTS

crooked

by Catherine Trieschmann
directed by Mike Bradwell

3 May - 3 June

'I mean, the fact that Jesus chose to turn the water into wine, rather than just decontaminating it, proves that drinking alcohol is not a sin'

Laney arrives in Oxford, Mississippi, an outsider with a twisted back and only her writing to keep her company. When she befriends the hapless born-again Maribel, Laney's penchant for story-telling soon spirals out of control.

A gloriously funny sideways glance at evangelical and Sapphic love way down south...

With Debbie Chazen, Amanda Hale and Suzan Sylvester

The Bush Theatre
Shepherds Bush Green, London W12 8QD
Nearest Tube: Shepherds Bush (Central Line) or Goldhawk Road (Hammersmith and City Line)

Box Office: 020 7610 4224
www.bushtheatre.co.uk

MOTORTOWN

by **Simon Stephens**

Cast in order of appearance
Lee **Tom Fisher**
Danny **Daniel Mays**
Marley **Daniela Denby-Ashe**
Tom **Steve Hansell**
Paul **Richard Graham**
Jade **Ony Uhiara**
Justin **Nick Sidi**
Helen **Fenella Woolgar**

Director **Ramin Gray**
Lighting Designer **Jean Kalman**
Sound Designer **Ian Dickinson**
Choreography **Hofesh Shechter**
Assistant Director **Hannah Eidinow**
Casting **Lisa Makin**
Production Manager **Paul Handley**
Stage Manager **Heidi Lennard**
Deputy Stage Manager **Emma Cameron**
Assistant Stage Manager **Jo Strickland**
Costumes **Iona Kenrick, Jackie Orton**

THE COMPANY

Simon Stephens (writer)
For the Royal Court: Country Music, Herons,
Bluebird (Choice Festival 1998).
Other theatre includes: On the Shores of the Wide
World (Royal Exchange & National Theatre);
Christmas (Bush); One Minute (ATC); Port (Royal
Exchange, Manchester).
Radio includes: Five Letters Home to Elizabeth,
Digging.
Awards include: Olivier Award for Best Play 2005
(On the Shores of the Wide World), Pearson
Award for Best Play 2001 (Port), Pearson Bursary
at the Royal Exchange, Manchester, Arts Council
Resident Dramatist at the Royal Court in 2000.

Daniela Denby-Ashe
Theatre includes: Sweet Panic (Duke of York); Les
Liaisons Dangereuses (Liverpool Playhouse); Shiver
Breathing (National Theatre).
Television includes: The Family Man, My Family,
North and South, Girls Weekend, Rescue Me,
Office Gossip, Is Harry on the Boat, Fish,
EastEnders, Kevin & Co., Absolutely Fabulous.
Radio includes: After the Affair, Baldi IV, Ring
Around the Bath, Head Over Heels.

Ian Dickinson (sound designer)
For the Royal Court: Rainbow Kiss, The Winterling,
Alice Trilogy, Fewer Emergencies, Way to Heaven,
The Woman Before, Stoning Mary (& Drum
Theatre, Plymouth), Breathing Corpses, Wild East,
Dumb Show, Shining City (& Gate, Dublin), Lucky
Dog, Blest Be the Tie (with Talawa), Ladybird, Notes
on Falling Leaves, Loyal Women, The Sugar
Syndrome, Blood, Playing the Victim (with Told By
an Idiot), Fallout, Flesh Wound, Hitchcock Blonde
(& Lyric), Black Milk, Crazyblackmuthafuckin'self,
Caryl Churchill Shorts, Push Up, Fucking Games,
Herons.
Other theatre includes: Pillars of the Community
(NT); A Few Good Men (Haymarket); Port, As You
Like It, Poor Superman, Martin Yesterday, Fast Food,
Coyote Ugly (Royal Exchange, Manchester); Night
of the Soul (RSC/Barbican); Eyes of the Kappa
(Gate); Crime & Punishment in Dalston (Arcola);
Search & Destroy (New End); The Whore's Dream
(RSC/Edinburgh).
Ian is Head of Sound at the Royal Court.

Tom Fisher
For the Royal Court: The Lying Kind, The Glory of
Living.
Other theatre includes: Hansel & Gretel (Lyric,
Hammersmith); 52 Revolutions (Oxford Stage
Company, Whitehall Theatre); Leonce and Lena, The
Great Highway, Lovers(Gate); Comedy of Errors

(RSC); Mirandolina (Lyric Hammersmith).
Television includes: Margaret, To the Ends of the
Earth, Foyles War, Casualty, North Square, Active
Defence.
Film includes: Amazing Grace, The Illusionist, Van
Helsing, Shanghai Knights, Club le Monde, The
Mummy Returns, Enigma, The Truth Game, The
Nine Lives of Thomas Katz, Simon Magus, Survive
Picasso, Crimetime.

Richard Graham
Theatre includes: Enemy of the People, Romeo a
Juliet (Young Vic); Boys Mean Business (Bush); A
Little Like Drowning (Hampstead); two seasons
Glasgow Citizens.
Television includes: Rockface, I Was a Rat,
Lockstock, Silent Witness, The Thing About Vince
The Passion, Maisie Raine, Real Women, The Fou
Floor, Olly's Prison, Time After Time.
Film includes: Vera Drake, Arthur's Dyke, Gangs
New York, 24 Hours in London, Bravo Two Zero
Titanic, Hostile Waters, ID, My Beautiful Laundre
In the Name of the Father, The Bounty, Under
Suspicion, An Ungentlemanly Act.

Ramin Gray (director)
For the Royal Court: Way to Heaven, Bear Hug,
The Weather, Ladybird, Advice to Iraqi Women,
Terrorism, Night Owls, Just a Bloke, Push Up, H
I Ate a Dog.
Other theatre includes: The American Pilot (RS
The Child, The Invisible Woman (Gate); Cat and
Mouse (Sheep) (Théâtre National de l'Odéon,
Paris/Gate); Autumn and Winter (Man in the
Moon); A Message for the Broken-Hearted
(Liverpool Playhouse/BAC); At Fifty She Discov
the Sea, Harry's Bag, Pig's Ear, A View from the
Bridge (Liverpool Playhouse); The Malcontent
(Latchmere).
Ramin is an Associate Director of the Royal Co

Steve Hansell
Theatre includes: Volpone (Present Moment
Theatre Company); The Man Who Needed To
Become Peter Cushing's Wife (Latchmere Thea
503); Mother Courage (Palace Theatre, Watford
Story Pimp, Holy Days (Black Sheep Comedy);
Macbeth (Lyric Studio, Hammersmith); Man Tra
(Menagerie); The Father (Empty Space
Productions); My England, Ooh Aah Showab Kh
Kicking Out (Arc Theatre Ensemble).
Television includes: Friday Night Project, Under
Moon, Round London.
Radio includes: Kicking Out.
Film includes: X-ED.

Jean Kalman (lighting designer)
For the Royal Court: Blasted, Lucky Dog.
Other theatre includes: The Cherry Orchard, The
Mahabharata, Woza Albert, The Tempest, Tourist
Guide, Undivine Comedy, Jacob Lenz, Golem, The
Hypochondriac (Almeida); Festen (Almeida & West
End); Richard III, White Chameleon, Night of the
Iguana, Macbeth, Prince's Play, King Lear, The Good
Person of Setzuan, A Midsummer Night's Dream,
The Powerbook (RNT); Electra, Hedda Gabler,
Coriolanus (Saltzburg); The Waste Land (Paris, New
York, London); Romeo and Juliet, Julius Caesar,
Little Eyolf, Pericles (RSC).
Opera with Robert Carsen includes: Turandot, La
Boheme, Madame Butterfly, Trittico (De Vlaamse
Opera, Antwerp); Semele (Aix-en-Provence
Festival/ENO), Nabucco, Alcina, Les Contes
d'Hoffman (Opera National de Paris), Eugene
Onegin (Metropolitan Opera, New York), Dialogue
des Carmelites (Amsterdam Opera/La Scala).
Other opera includes: Impression de Pelleas, Don
Giovanni, La Traviata, Turn of the Screw (Royal
Opera House); Wozzeck, Magic Flute (Opera
North); Don Giovanni, La Clemenza di Tito
(Glyndebourne); Il Ritorno d'Ulisse in Patria,
L'Incoronazione di Poppea, Orfeo ed Euridice, La
Boheme, Alceste; Don Giovanni (Munich); The
Cunning Little Vixen (Paris); Der Rosenkavalier
(ENO); Dialogue des Carmelites (Saito Kinen
Festival and Opera de Paris); Il Ritorno d'Ulisse in
Patria (Aix-en-Provence Festival); Alice (De
Nederlandse Opera); Lady Macbeth of Mtsensk
(Opera Australia); TEA (Suntory Hall and De
Nederlandse Opera).
Awards include: Lawrence Olivier award for
Richard III and nominated for White Chameleon
and A Midsummer Night's Dream.

Daniel Mays
For the Royal Court: The Winterling, Ladybird, The
One with the Oven, Just a Bloke.
Other theatre includes: M.A.D. (Bush).
Television includes: Funland, Class of '76, Top
Buzzer, Beneath the Skin, Keen Eddie, Tipping the
Velvet, Bodily Harm, NCS, Dead Casual, Manchild,
In Deep, Eastenders, The Bill.
Film includes: Middletown, A Good Year, Secret Life
of Words, Vera Drake, Best Man, Rehab, All or
Nothing, Pearl Harbor.
Awards include: Palmare-Reims Television Festival
2004 - Best Actor (for Rehab).

Hofesh Shechter (choreography)
Hofesh is a graduate of the Jerusalem Academy of
Dance, Israel, and is currently Associate Artist at
The Place, London.
Choreography includes: Fragments (Resolution!

2004 Festival/tour); Cult, Uprising (The Place)
Awards include: First Prize for the Serge Diaghiler
Choreography Competition, Audience Award for
The Place Prize 2004, Robin Howard Foundation
Commission 2006.

Nick Sidi
For the Royal Court: The Mother, Hustlers.
Other theatre includes: Tales from the Vienna
Woods (National Theatre); Port, As You Like It,
Bring Me Sunshine (Royal Exchange); Observe the
Sons of Ulster (Pleasance); Lucifer and the Lord,
The Nativity (Young Vic); Twelfth Night (Liverpool
Playhouse); The Colonel Bird (Gate); She's Electric
(Theatre Absolute).
Television includes: Vincent, Hotel Babylon, Bodies,
Silent Witness, Wire in the Blood, Blue Murder, No
Angels, Trust, Clocking Off, Stan the Man, The
Stretford Wives, Bob & Rose, Murder in Mind, City
Central, Passion Killers, Cold Feet, This Life.
Film includes: Scenes of a Sexual Nature.

Ony Uhiara
For the Royal Court: Fallout.
Other theatre includes: Walk Hard Talk Loud
(Tricycle); The Seer, Medea (West Yorkshire
Playhouse).
Television includes: Doctors, Rosemary & Thyme,
The Bill, A Proof 2, Holby City, Snowman, MIT, The
Crouches, Waking the Dead, The Vice V.
Film includes: Venus, Sixty 6.

Fenella Woolgar
Theatre includes: Bronte, Passage to India (Shared
Experience); A Midsummer Night's Dream, As You
Like It (Royal Exchange); The Miser (Salisbury
Playhouse); The Cherry Orchard (Theatre Royal
York); How the Other Half Loves (Palace Theatre,
Watford); Charlie's Aunt (Sheffield Crucible); Way
Up Stream (Derby Playhouse); Playboy of the
Western World (Bristol Old Vic).
Television includes: Mr Loveday's Little Outing, He
Knew He Was Right, Eroica, The Way We Live Now,
People Like Us.
Film includes: Untitled Woody Allen, Wah Wah, Vera
Drake, Stage Beauty, Bright Young Things.

THE ENGLISH STAGE COMPANY AT THE ROYAL COURT

The English Stage Company at the Royal Court opened in 1956 as a subsidised theatre producing new British plays, international plays and some classical revivals.

The first artistic director George Devine aimed to create a writers' theatre, 'a place where the dramatist is acknowledged as the fundamental creative force in the theatre and where the play is more important than the actors, the director, the designer'. The urgent need was to find a contemporary style in which the play, the acting, direction and design are all combined. He believed that 'the battle will be a long one to continue to create the right conditions for writers to work in'.

Devine aimed to discover 'hard-hitting, uncompromising writers whose plays are stimulating, provocative and exciting'. The Royal Court production of John Osborne's Look Back in Anger in May 1956 is now seen as the decisive starting point of modern British drama and the policy created a new generation of British playwrights. The first wave included John Osborne, Arnold Wesker, John Arden, Ann Jellicoe, N F Simpson and Edward Bond. Early seasons included new international plays by Bertolt Brecht, Eugène Ionesco, Samuel Beckett, Jean-Paul Sartre and Marguerite Duras.

The theatre started with the 400-seat proscenium arch Theatre Downstairs, and in 1969 opened a second theatre, the 60-seat studio Theatre Upstairs. Some productions transfer to the West End, such as Terry Johnson's Hitchcock Blonde, Caryl Churchill's Far Away and Conor McPherson's The Weir. Recent touring productions include Sarah Kane's 4.48 Psychosis (US tour) and Ché Walker's Flesh Wound (Galway Arts Festival). The Royal Court also co-produces plays which transfer to the West End or tour internationally, such as Conor McPherson's Shining City (with Gate Theatre, Dublin), Sebastian Barry's The Steward of Christendom and Mark Ravenhill's Shopping and Fucking (with Out of Joint), Martin McDonagh's The Beauty Queen Of Leenane (with Druid), Ayub Khan Din's East is East (with Tamasha).

Since 1994 the Royal Court's artistic policy has again been vigorously directed to finding and producing a new generation of playwrights. The writers include Joe Penhall, Rebecca Prichard, Michael Wynne, Nick Grosso, Judy Upton, Meredith Oakes, Sarah Kane, Anthony Neilson, Judith Johnson, James Stock, Jez Butterworth, Marina Carr, Phyllis Nagy, Simon Block, Martin McDonagh, Mark Ravenhill, Ayub Khan Din, Tamantha Hammerschlag, Jess Walters, Ché Walker,

photo: Andy Chopping

Conor McPherson, Simon Stephens, Richard Bean, Roy Williams, Gary Mitchell, Mick Mahoney, Rebecca Gilman, Christopher Shinn, Kia Corthron, David Gieselmann, Marius von Mayenburg, David Eldridge, Leo Butler, Zinnie Harris, Grae Cleugh, Roland Schimmelpfennig, Chloe Moss, DeObia Oparei, Enda Walsh, Vassily Sigarev, the Presnyakov Brothers, Marcos Barbosa, Lucy Prebble, John Donnelly, Clare Pollard, Robin French, Elyzabeth Gregory Wilder, Rob Evans, Laura Wade, Debbie Tucker Green and Simon Farquhar. This expanded programme of new plays has been made possible through the support of A.S.K. Theater Projects and the Skirball Foundation, The Jerwood Charity, the American Friends of the Royal Court Theatre and (in 1994/5 and 1999) the National Theatre Studio.

In recent years there have been record-breaking productions at the box office, with capacity houses for Joe Penhall's Dumb Show, Conor McPherson's Shining City, Roy Williams' Fallout and Terry Johnson's Hitchcock Blonde.

The refurbished theatre in Sloane Square opened in February 2000, with a policy still inspired by the first artistic director George Devine. The Royal Court is an international theatre for new plays and new playwrights, and the work shapes contemporary drama in Britain and overseas.

The Royal Court's long and successful history of innovation has been built by generations of gifted and imaginative individuals. In 2006, the company is celebrating its 50th Anniversary. The event is an important landmark for the performing arts in Britain and the company plans to deliver an extraordinary year of celebration and commemoration. For information on the many exciting ways you can help support the theatre, please contact the Development Department on 020 7565 5079.

artin McDonagh won the 1996 George Devine
ward, the 1996 Writers' Guild Best Fringe Play
ward, the 1996 Critics' Circle Award and the
'96 Evening Standard Award for Most Promising
aywright for The Beauty Queen of Leenane.
arina Carr won the 19th Susan Smith Blackburn
ize (1996/7) for Portia Coughlan. Conor
cPherson won the 1997 George Devine Award,
e 1997 Critics' Circle Award and the 1997
ening Standard Award for Most Promising
aywright for The Weir. Ayub Khan Din won the
'97 Writers' Guild Awards for Best West End Play
d New Writer of the Year and the 1996 John
hiting Award for East is East (co-production with
masha).

artin McDonagh's The Beauty Queen of Leenane
o-production with Druid Theatre Company) won
ur 1998 Tony Awards including Garry Hynes for
st Director. Eugene Ionesco's The Chairs
o-production with Theatre de Complicite) was
minated for six Tony awards. David Hare won
e 1998 Time Out Live Award for Outstanding
hievement and six awards in New York including
e Drama League, Drama Desk and New York
itics Circle Award for Via Dolorosa. Sarah Kane
n the 1998 Arts Foundation Fellowship in
aywriting. Rebecca Prichard won the 1998 Critics'
rcle Award for Most Promising Playwright for
rd Gal (co-production with Clean Break).

nor McPherson won the 1999 Olivier Award for
st New Play for The Weir. The Royal Court won
e 1999 ITI Award for Excellence in International
eatre. Sarah Kane's Cleansed was judged Best
reign Language Play in 1999 by Theater Heute in
ermany. Gary Mitchell won the 1999 Pearson
st Play Award for Trust. Rebecca Gilman was
nt winner of the 1999 George Devine Award
d won the 1999 Evening Standard Award for
ost Promising Playwright for The Glory of Living.

1999, the Royal Court won the European
eatre prize New Theatrical Realities, presented at
ormina Arte in Sicily, for its efforts in recent
ars in discovering and producing the work of
ung British dramatists.

y Williams and Gary Mitchell were joint
nners of the George Devine Award 2000 for
ost Promising Playwright for Lift Off and The
rce of Change respectively. At the Barclays
eatre Awards 2000 presented by the TMA,
chard Wilson won the Best Director Award for
vid Gieselmann's Mr Kolpert and Jeremy
erbert won the Best Designer Award for Sarah
ne's 4.48 Psychosis. Gary Mitchell won the
ening Standard's Charles Wintour Award 2000
r Most Promising Playwright for The Force of
ange. Stephen Jeffreys' I Just Stopped by to See
e Man won an AT&T: On Stage Award 2000.

David Eldridge's Under the Blue Sky won the Time
Out Live Award 2001 for Best New Play in the
West End. Leo Butler won the George Devine
Award 2001 for Most Promising Playwright for
Redundant. Roy Williams won the Evening
Standard's Charles Wintour Award 2001 for Most
Promising Playwright for Clubland. Grae Cleugh
won the 2001 Olivier Award for Most Promising
Playwright for Fucking Games.

Richard Bean was joint winner of the George
Devine Award 2002 for Most Promising Playwright
for Under the Whaleback. Caryl Churchill won the
2002 Evening Standard Award for Best New Play
for A Number. Vassily Sigarev won the 2002
Evening Standard Charles Wintour Award for Most
Promising Playwright for Plasticine. Ian MacNeil
won the 2002 Evening Standard Award for Best
Design for A Number and Plasticine. Peter Gill won
the 2002 Critics' Circle Award for Best New Play
for The York Realist (English Touring Theatre). Ché
Walker won the 2003 George Devine Award for
Most Promising Playwright for Flesh Wound. Lucy
Prebble won the 2003 Critics' Circle Award and
the 2004 George Devine Award for Most
Promising Playwright, and the TMA Theatre Award
2004 for Best New Play for The Sugar Syndrome.

Richard Bean won the 2005 Critics' Circle Award
for Best New Play for Harvest. Laura Wade won
the 2005 Critics' Circle Award for Most Promising
Playwright and the 2005 Pearson Best Play Award
for Breathing Corpses. The 2006 Whatsonstage
Theatregoers' Choice Award for Best New Play
was won by My Name is Rachel Corrie.

The 2005 Evening Standard Special Award was
given to the Royal Court 'for making and changing
theatrical history this last half century'.

ROYAL COURT BOOKSHOP

The Royal Court bookshop offers a range of
contemporary plays and publications on the theory
and practice of modern drama. The staff specialise
in assisting with the selection of audition
monologues and scenes. Royal Court playtexts from
past and present productions cost £2.

The Bookshop is situated in the downstairs
ROYAL COURT BAR.

Monday–Friday 3–10pm
Saturday 2.30–10pm
For information tel: 020 7565 5024
or email: bookshop@royalcourttheatre.com

PROGRAMME SUPPORTERS

The Royal Court (English Stage Company Ltd) receives its principal funding from Arts Council England, London. It is also supported financially by a wide range of private companies, charitable and public bodies, and earns the remainder of its income from the box office and its own trading activities.

The Genesis Foundation supports the Royal Court's work with International Playwrights.

Archival recordings of the Royal Court's Anniversary year made possible by Francis Finlay.

The Skirball Foundation funds a Playwrights' Programme at the theatre. The Artistic Directc Chair is supported by a lead grant from The Pe Jay Sharp Foundation, contributing to the activi of the Artistic Director's office. Over the past years the BBC has supported the Gerald Chap Fund for directors.

The Jerwood Charity supports new plays by n playwrights through the Jerwood New Playwri series.

ROYAL COURT
SLOANE SQUARE

3 June – 15 July 2006
Jerwood Theatre Downstairs

ROCK 'N' ROLL
by Tom Stoppard

direction **Trevor Nunn**
design **Rob Jones**
lighting **Howard Harrison**
sound **Ian Dickinson**
cast includes **Brian Cox,
Sinead Cusack, Rufus Sewell**

Tom Stoppard's provocative new play is his first for the Royal Court. Rock 'n' Roll spans the recent history of Czechoslovakia between the Prague Spring and the Velvet Revolution – but from the double perspective of Prague, where a rock 'n' roll band came to symbolise resistance to the regime, and the British left, represented by a Communist philosopher at Cambridge.

12 May – 10 June 2006
Jerwood Theatre Upstairs

DYING CITY
by Christopher Shinn

direction **James Macdonald**
design/lighting **Peter Mumford**
cast includes **Andrew Scott**

When one man goes to war he leaves the city, his wife and brother. A year later only the wife and brother remain.

Christopher Shinn's new play asks what happens when people and events apparently thousands of miles away affect the heart and soul of a city.

BOX OFFICE 020 7565 5000
BOOK ONLINE
www.royalcourttheatre.com

JERWOOD
NEW PLAYWRIGHTS

Since 1994 Jerwood New Playwrights has contributed to 53 new plays at the Royal Court including Joe Penhall's SOME VOICES, Mark Ravenhill's SHOPPING AND FUCKING (co-production with Out of Joint), Ayub Khan Din's EAST IS EAST (co-production with Tamasha), Martin McDonagh's THE BEAUTY QUEEN OF LEENANE (co-production with Druid Theatre Company), Conor McPherson's THE WEIR, Nick Grosso's REAL CLASSY AFFAIR, Sarah Kane's 4.48 PSYCHOSIS, Gary Mitchell's THE FORCE OF CHANGE, David Eldridge's UNDER THE BLUE SKY, David Harrower's PRESENCE, Simon Stephens' HERONS, Roy Williams' CLUBLAND, Leo Butler's REDUNDANT, Michael Wynne's THE PEOPLE ARE FRIENDLY, David Greig's OUTLYING ISLANDS, Zinnie Harris' NIGHTINGALE AND CHASE, Grae Cleugh's FUCKING GAMES, Rona Munro's IRON, Richard Bean's UNDER THE WHALEBACK, Ché Walker's FLESH WOUND, Roy Williams' FALLOUT, Mick Mahoney's FOOD CHAIN, Ayub Khan Din's NOTES ON FALLING LEAVES, Leo Butler's LUCKY DOG, Simon Stephens' COUNTRY MUSIC, Laura Wade's BREATHING CORPSES, Debbie Tucker Green's STONING MARY, David Eldridge's INCOMPLETE AND RANDOM ACTS OF KINDNESS, and Gregory Burke's ON TOUR.

In 2006, Jerwood New Playwrights are supporting O GO MY MAN by Stella Feehily, MOTORTOWN by Simon Stephens and RAINBOW KISS by Simon Farquhar.

The Jerwood Charitable Foundation is a registered charity dedicated to imaginative and responsible funding of the arts and other areas of human endeavour and excellence.

Leo Butler's LUCKY DOG
(photo: Ivan Kyncl)

David Eldridge's INCOMPLETE AND RANDOM
ACTS OF KINDNESS
(photo: Keith Pattison)

FOR THE ROYAL COURT

Artistic Director **Ian Rickson**
Associate Director International **Elyse Dodgson**
Associate Director **Ramin Gray**
Associate Director Casting **Lisa Makin**
Associate Director (50th) **Emily McLaughlin+**
Associate Directors* **Stephen Daldry, Marianne Elliott, James Macdonald, Katie Mitchell, Max Stafford-Clark, Richard Wilson**
Literary Manager **Graham Whybrow**
Literary Associate **Terry Johnson***
Voice Associate **Patsy Rodenburg***
Casting Deputy **Amy Ball**
International Associate **Orla O'Loughlin**
International Administrator **Chris James**
Trainee Director (C4 TDS) **Elina Männi§**
Artistic Assistant **Rebecca Hanna-Grindall**

Production Manager **Paul Handley**
Deputy Production Manager **Sue Bird**
Production Assistant **Sarah Davies**
Head of Lighting **Johanna Town**
Lighting Deputy **Greg Gould**
Lighting Assistants **Nicki Brown, Kelli Marston**
Lighting Board Operator **Stephen Andrews**
Head of Stage **Steven Stickler**
Stage Deputy **Daniel Lockett**
Stage Chargehand **Lee Crimmen**
Head of Sound **Ian Dickinson**
Sound Deputy **Emma Laxton**
Sound Assistant **David McSeveney**
Head of Costume **Iona Kenrick**
Costume Deputy **Jackie Orton**

YOUNG WRITERS PROGRAMME
Associate Director **Ola Animashawun**
Administrator **Nina Lyndon**
Outreach Worker **Lucy Dunkerley**
Education Officer **Laura McCluskey***
Writers' Tutor **Leo Butler***

General Manager **Diane Borger**
Administrator **Ollie Rance**
Finance Director **Sarah Preece**
Finance Officer **Rachel Harrison***
Finance Officer **Martin Wheeler**
Finance Manager **Helen Perryer**
Admin Assistant **Steve Pidcock**

Head of Press **Ewan Thomson**
Press Associate **Tamsin Treverton Jones**
Press Officer **Lyndsay Roberts**
Advertising and Marketing Agency **aka**
Marketing Consultant **Kym Bartlett**
Sales Manager **Neil Grutchfield**
Deputy Sales Manager **David Kantounas**
Box Office Sales Assistant **Helen Bennett, Stuart Grey, Samantha Preston**
Marketing Assistant **Gemma Frayne**
Press and Marketing Intern **Natalie Trangmar**

Head of Development **Nicky Jones**
Development Manager **Leona Felton**
Trusts and Foundations Manager **Gaby Styles**
Sponsorship Officer **Natalie Moss**
Development Assistant **Tiffany Knight**
Development Intern **Leila Bagnall**

Theatre Manager **Bobbie Stokes**
Front of House Manager **Nathalie Meghriche**
Restaurant Manager **Guy Halliday**
Duty House Managers **David Duchin, Charlie Revell, Matt Wood***
Bookshop Manager **Simon David**
Assistant Bookshop Manager **Edin Suljic***
Bookshop Assistants **Nicki Welburn*, Fiona Clift***
Stage Door/Reception **Simon David, Jon Hunter, Paul Lovegrove, Tyrone Lucas**

Thanks to all of our box office assistants, ushers and bar staff.

+ The Associate Director post is supported by the BBC through the Gerald Chapman Fund.

§ This theatre is supported by The Harold Hyam Wingate Foundation under the Channel 4 Theatre Director Scheme.

* Part-time.

ENGLISH STAGE COMPANY

President
Sir John Mortimer CBE QC

Vice President
Dame Joan Plowright CBE

Honorary Council
Sir Richard Eyre CBE
Alan Grieve CBE
Martin Paisner CBE

Council
Chairman **Anthony Burton**
Vice Chairwoman **Liz Calder**

Members
Judy Daish
Graham Devlin
Sir David Green KCMG
Joyce Hytner OBE
Tamara Ingram
Stephen Jeffreys
Phyllida Lloyd
James Midgley
Edward Miliband MP
Sophie Okonedo
Katharine Viner

We've always been happy to be less famous than our clients

Motortown

'For something to begin something has to end
The first sign of hope is despair
The first sign of the new is terror'

Heiner Müller, *Mauser*
(translated by Marc von Henning)

Characters

Lee
Danny
Marley
Tom
Paul
Jade
Justin
Helen

The play should be performed as far as possible without décor.

I am indebted to Ian Rickson for all his support over the past seven years, and in particular for his inspiration in the writing of this play. I am indebted too to Ramin Gray and Marianne Elliott and Graham Whybrow and Ola Animashawun and Nina Lyndon and all the rest of the staff and writers of the Royal Court Young Writers' programme. And to Mel Kenyon. I am grateful to the British Council and to Mark Amery and Playmarket, New Zealand, for all of their support in the beginning of 2006 and all of the writers and actors I worked with there. Thanks to Chris Mead for the quote.

This play owes a massive amount to the spirit of B. R. Wallers and The Country Teasers.

Happy Anniversary Princess Sarah.

This play is for Oscar and for Stan and also for Mark.

SWS,
Gothenberg, March 2006

Scene One

Danny *and* **Lee**.

Lee   She doesn't want to see you. She told me to tell you.

A brief pause.

She told me to tell you that you were frightening her. Your letters were frightening, she said.

A brief pause.

I'm really, really, really, really sorry.

A very, very long pause. The two brothers look at each other. Then **Danny** *looks away. He moves away from* **Lee**.

Lee   You sleep all right?

Danny   I did. Thank you.

Lee   That's good.

Danny   I had some extraordinary dreams.

Lee   Did yer?

Danny   I did, yes.

Lee   What about?

Danny   I can't remember, to be honest. I say that. I'm not entirely sure if it's true. I'm not sure if it's that I can't remember or I can't quite believe them, yer with me? My dreams! I'm telling yer! What time is it?

Lee   It's nine o'clock. I've been up for a while. I was waiting for yer.

Danny   Were yer?

Lee   I get up at five-thirty.

Danny   Do yer?

Lee   Most days.

Danny   Right. That's quite early, Lee.

Lee   Yes.

Danny   You should join the fucking army, mate.

Lee   Don't swear.

Danny   You what?

Lee   It's ignorant.

Beat.

Danny   That I was 'frightening' her? Are you sure that's what she said?

Lee   With your letters.

Danny   That's a bit of a surprise to me, I have to say.

A pause.

Lee   You sleep with a frown on your face. Did anybody ever tell you that?

Danny   No.

Lee   Well, it's true. I went in to check on you. You were frowning.

Danny   What have you been doing since half-five?

Lee   I was cleaning the flat.

Danny   Good idea.

Lee   Can I get you some breakfast?

Danny   That'd be lovely, Lee. Thank you.

Lee   I've got some Coco Pops. Would you like some Coco Pops or would you prefer Sugar Puffs?

Danny   Coco Pops is fine.

Lee   And a cup of tea?

Danny   Lovely.

Lee   With milk and two sugars and the tea bag in first before the hot water?

Danny   That's right.

Lee   Would you like some toast as well?

Danny   I would, please.

Lee   I've got butter, margarine, Marmite, jam, marmalade, peanut butter, honey, Nutella and lemon curd.

Danny   Butter would be nice. And a little bit of marmalade please.

Lee   Right. Coming right up!

He doesn't move.

Danny   How've you been, Lee?

Lee   I've been all right. I've been very good. I've been healthy. I had to clean up quite quietly while you were sleeping. But that isn't a problem.

Danny   Good.

Lee   And how are you?

Danny   I'm fine, mate. I'm fine. It's nice to be back.

Lee   I should have asked if you wanted to sleep in my bed.

Danny   No, you shouldn't have done.

Lee   I should have done. I just chose not to.

I passed my driving test.

Danny   Nice one. Well done. When was that?

Lee   In January. It was easy. Passed first time.

Danny   I should think so. I did too.

Lee   Did you?

Danny   At Pirbright.

Lee   You didn't tell me.

Danny   We should get a car. Shouldn't we?

Lee   Yeah.

Danny   Put it in the driveway. Give it a clean. Show it off. You could wear a suit. Get a cup of tea in the morning. Go to work. With yer tie on. You'd love that, wouldn't you?

Lee   Ha!

Danny   How *are* Mum and Dad?

Lee   They're very well, thank you. I think they're pleased you're home.

Danny   Great.

Lee   They talk about you incessantly. It's like a kind of water torture for visitors.

Danny   I can imagine.

Lee   You gonna go and see them, you think?

Danny   I don't think so, no.

Lee   Right. Why?

Danny   I don't think I really want to, Lee, that's all.

Lee   I ironed your shirts for you. While you were sleeping. And after I tidied up.

Danny   Right. Thank you.

Lee   That's all right. I like ironing. I'm really good at it.

He exits.

Danny *stands alone. Long pause.*

Lee *returns with a cup of tea for both of them.*

Lee   We saw you on telly. On the news. On *Newsnight*. I went round to Mum and Dad's. They videotaped it. (*He drinks his tea.*) It didn't look anything like you.

Danny   I've not seen it.

Lee   Well, go round then. Ask Mum and Dad. They'd definitely let you watch it. You'll be astonished. It's like you're a completely different person.

He leaves again. Comes back almost immediately.

I go round. They seem increasingly old to me. They're getting smaller. Their backs are arched. Their skin is getting wrinkly.

He leaves again. He comes back in with some toast, no plate. He passes the toast to **Danny**.

Danny   Thanks, Lee. This is smashing.

He eats, then looks at **Lee**, *who is watching him.*

Danny   London?

Lee (*immediately*)   7,465,209.

Danny   Paris?

Lee (*immediately*)   2,144,703.

Danny   Mexico City?

Lee (*immediately*)   8,605,239.

Danny *gives him a big smile.* **Lee** *smiles back, proud and shy.*

Lee   Were you all right out there then, Danny?

Danny   I was, it was fine.

Lee   You spent most of your time giving out chocolates from what I could tell. They seemed quite friendly.

Danny   They were. See their little faces light up. All big grins. A mouthful of fucking Mars bar and they're putty in yer hand, Lee, I'm telling yer.

Lee   You're gonna be on *Trisha* soon, you. Knowing you. I think.

Danny   Fuck off.

Lee   'My addiction to swearing and being a swear monkey!'

Danny   When did she come round?

Lee   Last week.

Danny   Where's she staying?

Lee   Up Goresbrook, behind the field.

Danny   In her old house?

Lee   I think so, Danny, yes. But she told me not to tell you that.

Danny   Right.

Lee   She seemed very sure about it.

Danny   Yeah.

Lee   See Denise Van Outen?

Danny   Yeah. What about her?

Lee   I'd like to *be* her.

Danny   You what?

Lee   Just thinking out loud. How's your breakfast?

Danny   It's fine thank you, Lee. It's lovely.

Lee   What are you going to do today?

Danny   I don't know.

Lee   We should do the washing up together. Bring back memories. For old times' sake.

Danny   We could do. What you reading?

Lee   You what?

Danny   At the moment.

Lee   I'm reading a true-life book about ghosts and haunted houses.

Danny   You're a big inspiration to me, Lee.

Lee *walks off. He comes back with a ghost book in his hands. Shows* **Danny** *a picture in it.*

Lee Have you seen this one? Back of the car. The car is a hearse. On the way to a funeral. And that woman, it's her funeral. Fake or real? Do you think?

Danny I don't know.

Lee Your hand's shaking.

Danny Yeah.

Lee It's always done that. What's that about, do you think?

Danny I don't know.

Lee West Ham got promoted.

Danny I heard.

Lee You missed it. And you missed my thirtieth birthday party.

Danny I was at the camp.

Lee It was a weekend. You stayed put. Watching *Grandstand*.

And you never, ever ring me, ever.

Did Degsie go out with you?

Danny Degsie?

Lee From the passing out.

Danny I don't think I knew anybody called Degsie.

Lee I talked to him at your passing out.

Danny I don't remember.

Lee He was from Goole, in Yorkshire. His father was a mechanic.

Danny I don't remember anybody called Degsie.

Lee Or Francis Stifford. Or Charlie Sturt? Did they go out with you?

Danny   How many people did you talk to at my passing out?

Lee   I –

Danny   You had a good day, that day, didn't you?

Lee   I did. It was great. I'm sorry about the Coco Pops. I feel like I've led you down the garden path. I've got no food in at all. I should have got some and I just didn't.

Danny   You still get your lunches?

Lee   Yeah.

Danny   They still bring them round?

Lee   Yeah. They do. Yeah.

Danny   Will they bring one round for me?

Lee   No. They won't.

Are you going to go out today, do you think?

Danny   I might do, Lee, yes.

Lee   I might go out today, too. After my lunch gets here.

Danny   We could fucking go out together.

Lee   I'm gonna start a swear box. I'll be able to buy a dishwasher by the end of it.

Danny   How much deodorant have you got on?

Lee   A bit.

Danny   Don't go fucking swimming, will yer?

Lee   Why?

Danny   You smell like a tart's boudoir!

Lee   Like a what?

Danny   Seriously. Show us yer teeth.

Lee   My teeth?

Danny   You wanna get them sorted Lee, they're fucking disgusting. Here. Have a Polo. Have two. Have another, save it for later.

Lee   I told her she should tell you herself.

Danny   Did yer?

Lee   At first I did, but then I promised.

Danny   Thanks.

Lee   I didn't know what to do really.

Danny   Don't worry about it.

Lee   I never liked her anyway.

Danny   No.

Lee   The way she spoke to me. She was really rude.

Pause. **Danny** *smiles at him.*

Danny   We should go for a day trip. Us two, I think.

Lee   A day trip?

Danny   Go up Southend. Go to the seaside. Get a few drinks at The Northview. Look out to sea. Go and ride on the fairground. I'd look after you. See you all right. Be good that, I think. Don't you think, Lee, wouldn't you like that?

Lee   Maybe. After lunch.

Danny   I don't know if I can wait until lunch-time.

Lee   I have to, they're coming round.

Pause.

Are you incredibly angry with me, about Marley?

Danny   No, Lee, I'm not.

Lee   It's not my fault, is it?

Danny   No.

Lee   Don't shoot the messenger they say, don't they?

Danny   They do, yeah.

Lee   I'm glad you're a soldier.

Danny   Thanks.

Lee   I'm glad you're brave.

Danny   Thanks.

Lee   But you're incredibly messy.

Danny (*with a chuckle*)   Sorry.

Lee   Why are you laughing at me?

Danny   I just enjoy you. And I've not seen you.

Lee   I hate the summer. I get a bit sweaty.

Danny   You know the thing about you, Lee?

Lee   What?

Danny   You can kind of hold stuff in a bit. I quite admire that, as it goes.

Lee   That's not true.

Danny   It is, you know.

Lee   I can't hold anything in, me. I can't even hold my farts in.

Danny   That wasn't what I was talking about.

Lee   No.

Danny   I'm not going to wait until after lunch.

Lee   Right.

Danny   I think I'm going to go out on my own. Have a wander.

Lee   Will you be home for your tea?

Danny   I think so.

Lee   Give me a ring. On the phone. If you won't.

Danny   Right.

Lee   Are you going to go and see Marley?

Danny   No. Not if she doesn't want me to.

Lee   It's just what she says.

Danny   Yeah.

Lee   We've not got the same hair. Or the same bone structure. Or the same eyes. Or anything. We did once. But now we don't.

Danny *looks at* **Lee** *for a long time.*

Danny   Will you be here when I get back?

Scene Two

Danny *and* **Marley**.

Danny Lee told me that you went to see him. He told me that you didn't want to see me any more. That you told him I was frightening you. Is that true, Marley?

No response.

Was I frightening you?

No response.

Was I frightening you, Marley? Were my letters frightening you?

Marley Calm down.

Danny I was writing you letters. They were letters, that's all.

Marley Calm down, Danny, people are starting to stare at you.

Danny Who is? Who's starting to stare at me?

Marley There's no need to shout. I'm sitting right here.

Danny If I was frightening you, then you could have told me yourself. You could have written to me. You could have come to see me. You didn't need to leave me a poxy message. I'm not sixteen anymore.

Marley –

Danny I never wanted to frighten you. It was never my intention to frighten you.

Marley All right.

Danny I had nobody else I knew I could write to.

Marley Fine.

Danny Don't say that.

Marley What?

Danny   Don't just sit there with your face screwed up like that. It's like you're passing a note through a classroom.

Marley   Danny, look, I'm glad you're back. I'm glad you're safe. I'm glad you didn't get your head blown off. I hope you're going to be okay.

Danny   I am.

Marley   But I don't owe you anything. And if I ask you to leave me alone, through your brother, or through a letter, or through a text message or a note via our teacher, then I expect you to leave me alone.

Danny   I'm gonna be more than all right. I'm gonna be great.

Marley   'Cause if you don't –

Danny   What?

Marley   I'll call the cops. I'll go to court. I'll get an order out on you, no danger.

Danny   You what?

Marley   I mean it, Danny.

A long pause. He stares at her. She has to break his stare.

Where you staying?

Danny   Where am I . . . ?

Marley   You heard me, where are you staying, Danny?

Danny   What do you wanna know that for?

Marley   You staying with your Mum and Dad?

Danny   No. I'm not. I'm staying at Lee's. What do you wanna know that for?

Marley   So I can tell the cops if you ever contact me again.

Danny   You're lying.

Marley   Try me.

Danny   You must be.

A pause. **Marley** *smiles.*

Marley   I saw your Lee a while back, as it goes. Having his driving lesson. Driving down the Heathway. He was driving at about twelve miles an hour. There was a big queue building up behind him.

Danny   Don't.

Marley   Why did you come and see me when I asked you not to?

Danny   Why do you think?

Marley   I have no idea.

A very long pause.

I'm gonna finish my tea.

Danny   Right.

Marley   And then I'm gonna go home.

A very long pause. She drinks her tea.

Danny   How is it?

Marley   What?

Danny   Your tea?

Marley   It's lovely.

Danny   That's good. Mine's a bit tepid. Should have tasted the tea we had out there. It was horrible.

Marley   I bet it was.

Danny   It was powdered.

Marley   Great!

Danny   It tasted like concrete.

Marley   Lovely.

Danny   I really missed you.

Marley   You said.

Danny   Is this going to be the last time I ever see you? 'Cause if it is I don't quite understand why.

Marley   Some of the things you said . . .

Danny   I don't remember.

Marley   I was only your girlfriend for about three months.

Danny   It was more than that.

Marley   And then you write that.

Danny   You have a way of talking to boys, did you know? It makes me want to smash their faces in.

Pause. He grins.

You got a boyfriend now?

Marley   Stop it.

Danny   Have you, Marley? Are you seeing somebody?

Marley   I don't believe this.

Danny   That means you have, doesn't it? Who is it, Marley? Who is he?

Marley   I'm going.

Danny   Marley, who is he? Do I know him?

Marley   See you, Danny.

Danny   Did he go to our sixth form?

Marley   Fuck off.

Danny   Don't. Don't, Marley. Please don't.

He goes to her. Grabs her arm.

Marley   Get off my arm.

He lets go of her.

Danny   Please don't go.

Marley   Fuck off.

Danny   Please, Marley, don't. I'm sorry. I just missed you, is all. If that's out of order then I take it all back.

Marley   I stopped being your girlfriend years ago.

Danny   It wasn't years.

Marley   I thought you were my friend.

Danny   Yeah.

Marley   There's nothing wrong with that. I was going to university. You were down in Pirbright. I thought we were mates.

Danny   Yeah. I know.

Marley   Your letters were really weird and they were really frightening. You really hurt my arm.

Danny   I'm sorry.

A very long pause.

I wish you'd come. To Pirbright. To see me. It was an amazing place. Better than anywhere round here by miles. I wish you'd come to the passing out. Lee came. He was an embarrassment. With his big old glasses on. Looking like a freak.

Marley   How long you gonna stay with him?

Danny   Not long.

Marley   Where are you gonna move to?

Danny   I have no idea.

Marley   Don't they sort you out with somewhere?

Danny   No. I paid myself out.

Marley   So they just leave you?

Danny   They do, yeah.

Marley   To fend for yourself?

Danny   Yeah.

Marley   Well, you should be good at that, shouldn't you? You're trained for that, aren't you, Danny? You could go to the Marshes. Dig a hole.

Danny   I could, yeah.

Marley   You'd love that, you, I bet.

Danny   I can lie awake at night and imagine what it's like to kiss your face.

Marley   Don't.

Danny   You can too, I bet.

Marley   This is ridiculous. You couldn't even get it up half the time. Could you, though? When you think about it. Came in about two seconds when you did.

Scene Three

Danny *and* **Tom.**

Tom I think people are more like flowers than we ever give them credit for.

Danny You what?

Tom See me, Danny. I'm a little flower. Bit of sunshine like this and I bloom, mate. Get outside. Put yer shorts on. You wanna do a bit of that.

Danny You reckon?

Tom I didn't think they'd let you out yet, Danny.

Danny Didn't yer?

Tom I thought you'd still be out there.

Danny I came home early.

Tom You had enough, had you?

Danny I had, a bit.

Tom How was it?

Danny It was easy.

Tom Pushing on an open door.

Danny Mostly it involved waiting around all fucking day. Do a couple of patrols.

Tom Give out a few Spangles.

Danny We stayed in the airport. They turned the Basra international airport into our base. Had these big old statues and fountains and marble floors and everything.

Tom Lovely.

Danny Had a PlayStation. Watch a few DVDs. Get yer one ginger beer a day.

I just got bored.

Came home.

Beat.

They smile at each other.

Tom   I'm glad you did.

Danny   Me too.

Tom   It's good to see yer.

Danny   Yeah. It's good to see you, too.

Tom   You want a crisp, Danny? They're sea salt and malt vinegar.

Danny   Lovely. Thank you.

Tom *looks at* **Danny** *for a long time.*

Tom   You staying with your Lee?

Danny   I am, yeah.

Tom   How is he, Lee?

Danny   He's fucking completely puddled. But he's not so bad. I quite like him. I'm on his couch.

Tom   Nice. You not going see your folks?

Danny   I don't think so, Tom, no.

Tom   They still up in Becontree, are they?

Danny   They are mate, yeah.

Tom   How come you're not gonna go and see them?

Danny   'Cause they do my fucking head in, Tom.

Tom   Do they?

Danny   They do, yeah.

Tom   Right. Right. Right. Right. Good. And have you seen Marley?

Danny   I haven't, Tom, no.

Tom   Best off out of that one, I reckon.

Danny   Yeah, me too.

Tom   I think she was completely insane.

Danny   I think you're right.

Tom   I saw you on the telly. With Paxo. I thought you looked all right. I thought you came off fairly well, as it goes.

Danny   Thanks, Tom.

Tom   Other people said they thought you looked a bit odd.

Danny   Did they?

Tom   Said it looked nothing like you. Are you as hard as fuck now?

Danny   You what?

Tom   Are you?

Danny   I don't know. I don't think so.

Tom   You look it, you know?

Danny   Thanks, Tom.

Tom   You look quite handsome, as it goes.

Danny   That's very kind of you.

Tom   In a kind of James Cagney kind of way.

Danny   James Cagney?

Tom   Definitely more James Cagney than Leonardo DiCaprio. What are you gonna do for money?

Danny   I'm all right for a bit.

Tom   You could come and work here, if you wanted.

Danny   Thanks, Tom. I'll be fine.

Tom   Work on the till. Count the cash. Place the orders. Any of that.

Danny   That's kind of you, mate.

Tom And have you got long-term plans?

Danny Not completely, no.

Tom I think you should look into a career in film special effects.

Danny Do yer?

Tom You'd be good at that, I think.

Danny You reckon?

Tom I do, yeah.

Danny How much is this, Tom?

Tom Thirty-five pounds. I could give it you for twenty-seven.

Danny Thank you.

Tom That's not a problem. You're a friend of mine. I'm happy to help you out.

It's a Walther P99 replica. Semi-automatic. There's no hammer, see? The trigger's beautiful, I think. Although it is odd at first. It has a very long, double-action first shot. But then it's very clean, for the rest of the magazine. You don't need to exert any pressure at all. It has a six-millimetre calibre. It takes 0.2 gram pellets. I can *give* you a hundred of those as part of the deal. It's a very authentic model, this one. Probably the most authentic I've got in just now.

Danny Right.

Tom I've got a good deal on the Smith and Wesson at the moment. Which is a simple six-shot. At twenty pounds. I've got a Taurus PT92 in chrome, which I think is actually rather elegant. That's thirty pounds to you. I've got a KWC Beretta for you at fifteen quid, Danny. 0.12 gram pellets, nearly hundred metres a second. If you fancy it we could take them out.

Danny Nice one.

Tom Go up home. Go up the Chase. Shoot some ducks.

Danny   We could do.

Tom   Mind you, you could probably get us on Foulness, couldn't you? Get on the Island.

Danny   I could try.

Tom   You ever been up there?

Danny   I haven't, Tom, no.

Tom   I'd fucking love to go there, me.

Danny   Yeah. I'll take this, Tom.

Tom   Good choice.

Danny   It's a good weight, eh?

Tom   It's a cop gun. Special forces. Undercover. James Bond type of thing.

Danny   Great.

Tom   You got cash?

Danny   I do, yeah.

Tom   Lovely.

Danny   I've not been up the Chase since I've got back.

Tom   I've not been for fucking years, mate.

Danny   It's changed, hasn't it? The whole town.

Tom   I can never tell any more.

Danny   It has, it's got worse, I think.

Tom   The factory's almost completely closed up now.

Danny   I heard. I went down. To get the train up here.

Tom   The whole of Chequers is all completely burnt out. All of it. The whole fucking street.

Danny   Yeah.

Tom   There's a whole new array of drugs you can get down there. Drugs I've never even heard of before. It's like a supermarket for drugs.

Danny   I'm half tempted to go up Eastbrook.

Tom   Are you?

Danny   Take this with me. 'All right, sir?' Bang!

Tom   Ha! Don't.

Danny   No. Don't worry, I won't.

Tom   I know what we should do!

Danny   What's that?

Tom   We should go up Shoeburyness. Take my car up. Do some doughnuts. I've not done that since you left. Or go Southend. Go cockle picking.

Danny   Yeah.

Tom   Have you got the new 50 Cent album?

Danny   I haven't Tom, no.

Tom   It's fucking great.

Danny   Is it?

Tom   What about the new Outcast?

Danny   No.

Tom   Snoop Dog?

Danny   I've not.

Tom   Black Eyed Peas?

Danny   No.

Tom   I've got all of them. Jay-Z, featuring Beyoncé?

Danny   No.

Tom   He's a lucky cunt, isn't he?

Danny   He is, yeah.

Tom   I'll burn 'em for you! Have you got an iPod?

Danny   No.

Tom   You should get one, I think.

Danny   Yeah, I will.

Tom   I've got 6,324 songs on mine. Mostly hip hop. I got some Rod Stewart, for me mum.

Danny   If I wanted it converted, would you know where I could go?

Tom   Sorry, Danny?

Danny   The P99, if I wanted it engineered, to fire live ammo, do you know anybody who could do that for me?

Scene Four

Danny, **Paul** *and* **Jade**.

Paul   To ask about the meaning of life is about as philosophically interesting as asking about the meaning of wood or the meaning of grass. There is no meaning. Life is, as science has proven in the last two years, a genetic system. An arrangement of molecular structure. There is no solidity. Only a perception of solidity. There is no substance. Only the perception of substance. There is no space. Only the perception of space. This is a freeing thing, in many ways, Danny. It means I can be anywhere. At any time. I can do anything. I just need to really try. This is Jade. Say hello, Jade.

Jade   Hello.

Danny   Hello.

Paul   How's Tom doing?

Danny   He's all right, I think.

Paul   Good man. Good man. Good man. He's a bit of a weird old cunt though, don't you think?

Danny   I do, sometimes.

Paul   He is. He speaks very highly of you, but he is a bit of a weird old cunt.

Danny (*to* **Jade**, *lying*)   Jade was my wife's name.

Paul   Are you married, Danny?

Danny   I was.

Paul   How old are you?

Danny   Twenty-seven.

Paul   What happened to your wife, Danny?

Danny   She got killed.

Paul   No.

Danny   We got robbed. She got shot in the chest.

Paul   Good God, Danny, that's awful.

Danny   Yeah.

Paul   When was this?

Danny   A couple of years ago.

Paul   Did they catch the fucker?

Danny   Yeah. He was a soldier. Some squaddie.

Paul   For God's sake. I'm really sorry to hear that. Aren't you, Jade? Aren't you sorry to hear that?

Jade   Yeah. I am.

Paul   We're both of us really sorry to hear that, Danny.

A long pause.

Yes.

Is it Danny or Daniel?

Danny   Danny.

Paul   Good. How boyish! What do you do, Danny?

Danny   What do I do?

Paul   Your job, what is it?

Danny   I'm in film. I do special effects for films.

Paul   Do you really? That's rather remarkable to me! What a remarkable job. What films have you done?

Danny   None that you know.

Paul   Go on. Try me. I go to the cinema all the time, don't I, Jade?

Jade   Yeah. He does.

Danny   I worked on a few of the Bond movies. I worked on the gun scenes on some of the Bond films.

Paul Which ones?

Danny *Die Another Day*. Mainly.

Paul I never saw that. Did I?

Jade No.

Paul I hate James Bond. I think his films are fucking dreadful. Did you come in on the train?

Danny I did, yeah.

Paul I like the train ride. Out of Dagenham.

Danny Yeah.

Paul I like Dagenham.

Danny Do yer?

Paul It's full of fat kids in football shirts, isn't it? Lovely that. I like it round here more, though. I like the views, you understand?

Danny I do.

Paul Canning Town. London, E16. Do you like London, Danny?

Danny I'm not sure.

Paul You're not sure?!

Danny It's a bit big for me.

Paul A bit big. (*He smiles.*) You see, that's the problem with the Essex native, though, Danny, isn't it? They never fucking leave.

Danny That's not completely true.

Paul What's the furthest you've ever been to?

Danny You what?

Paul In the world?

Danny France.

Paul Is it?

Danny Yeah.

Paul Ha!

Jade *smirks too.*

Danny Don't laugh.

Paul No. You're right. I'm being rude. I'm sorry. It's just I'm quite the traveller. I travel almost constantly. I'm more familiar with aeroplanes than I am with buses. That's actually the truth. Do you want to know something about aeroplanes?

Danny Go on.

Paul You know the real reason why people tell you to adopt the brace position in the event of an emergency on an aeroplane? It's so the impact of the crash on the neck forces the spinal column into the skull and into the brain and kills you immediately. Rather than allowing you to suffer a prolonged and horrible death. That's the reason why, really.

Danny This is my gun.

He pulls his gun out of his pocket and shows it to him.

Paul Yes. Put it away. We'll sort that out in a bit. Can I get you a cup of tea, Danny?

Danny No thank you.

Paul Or a coffee? Or a beer? A whisky? Anything like that?

Danny A water.

Paul A water? You want a glass of water? Tap or mineral?

Danny Tap.

Paul Tap water. Very good. Ice? Lemon?

Danny No thank you.

Paul As it comes, as it were. Terrific. Jade, sweetheart, get Danny a glass of water, will you? There's a good girl.

Jade *leaves. They watch her go.*

Paul   She's fourteen. You wouldn't think it to look at her, would yer?

Danny   I don't know.

Paul   You wouldn't. Immoral really, but . . .

A long pause. **Paul** *stares at* **Danny**.

Paul   Can I ask you this? Do you ever get that feeling? When you're in, you're in, you're in say a, a, a, a bar or a restaurant or walking down a street, and you see a girl. A teenage girl. You see the nape of her neck. In her school uniform. With her friends. All pigtailed. And you just want to reach out and touch. You ever get that?

Danny   I'm not sure.

Paul   You see, when you can't tell the difference any more between what is real and what is a fantasy. That's frightening, I think.

They don't let you take anything onto planes anymore, Danny. Did you know that? Since 9/11. Fucking nothing. Apart from pens, oddly. They should take pens off you. That's what I think. The pen can be a lethal instrument. You can stab somebody in the eye. Push it all the way in. Cripple them at least. Cut into the brain. Leave them brain-damaged. It'd be easy, that. I'd leave the end sticking out, wouldn't you?

Danny   I don't know.

Paul   You would. I would. It would look hilarious.

I need a shave.

You know what I think about 9/11, Danny?

Danny   No, I'm actually in a bit of a –

Paul   Wait for your fucking drink!

Danny

Paul *glares at him.*

Paul   The best heist film Hollywood never made. That's what I think. The level of planning, the level of daring, the downright fucking scientific sexiness and brass-balled braveness that went into that operation! Christ! You should tell your friends. They could cast it up! Cast Bruce Willis. Black him up a bit. That'd be a fucking blockbuster all right.

Danny   Yeah.

Paul   They should make films out of everything, I think. Films and musicals. They should make musicals out of everything as well. Imagine it! *Bulger! The Musical!* I'd pay forty quid to see that.

Jade *returns. She gives* **Danny** *a glass of water.*

Danny   Thank you very much.

Jade   That's all right.

Paul *waits for* **Danny** *to drink. Watches him.*

Paul   How is it? Your water?

Danny   It's fine, thanks.

Paul   Look out there. Have you the slightest idea how many tube lines run under the square mile area you can see from out of that window, Danny, have you? It's completely fucking hollow down there. Beneath the surface of the ground. It's full of vermin and metal. Rats. Mice. Squirrels. Foxes. Soon there'll be dogs fucking everywhere. Stray dogs. Little pit bulls. Wandering around. They'll come in down the river. And then, in the future, in London, people will find foxes in their living rooms. You'll have to batter them with your broom sticks. Or shoot them in the head. Either method works just as well. Scabby fucking things. They'll eat your cat as soon as look at you. I'm gonna bring hunting for foxes with hounds back. But not in fucking Surrey. Not in Wiltshire. Down Oxford Street. A huge fucking pack of us.

He makes the noise of a hunting trumpet.

Show me.

Danny *shows him his gun.*

Paul   P99. Nice. Let me have a look.

He opens a small toolkit, takes out a tiny screwdriver and a tape measure and opens the gun. Goes to work adjusting it. He wears half-moon spectacles as he does so.

The notion of a War on Terror is completely ingenious. It is now possible to declare war on an abstraction. On an emotional state.

He continues to work.

God. Law. Money. The left. The right. The church. The state. All of them lie in tatters. Wouldn't you be frightened?

He continues to work.

The only thing we can do is feast ourselves on comfort foods and gobble up television images. Sport has never been more important. The family unit seems like an act of belligerence. *All* long-term relationships are doomed or ironic. Therefore sexuality must be detached. But, because of fucking AIDS, detached sexuality is suicidal. So everybody goes online.

Hardcore black fucking MPEG porn . . . junky lesbian breast torture . . . bondage fantasies, hardcore pics . . . free bestiality stories, low-fat diet, free horse-sex, torture victims zoo . . .

Marvellous stuff!

You can get all the free trailers. And that's enough for me. I wouldn't spend any fucking money on it. That's just a waste, I think. I think that's when you're addicted to it.

He continues to work.

I saw a fifty-year-old man sit a sixteen-year-old Brummie girl on his lap. He held her breast in his hand and got her to smile at the webcam. Asked her what she thought all of the people watching did while she masturbated. She said she thought they masturbated. It was a truthful image. It sits in my consciousness.

He looks up at **Danny** *and points with his tiny screwdriver.*

Paul   You want to know the truth about the poor in this country? They're not cool. They're not soulful. They're not honest. They're not the salt of the fucking earth. They're thick. They're myopic. They're violent. They're drunk most of the time. They like shit music. They wear shit clothes. They tell shit jokes. They're racist, most of them, and homophobic the lot of them. They have tiny parameters of possibility and a minuscule spirit of enquiry or investigation. They would be better off staying in their little holes and fucking each other. And killing each other.

They're on the way there already, of course. There's a guy who lives downstairs. He got himself involved in all that. Couple of fellahs come along. Cut his biceps in half with a pair of garden shears. Absolutely extraordinary.

Every week entire towns are torn apart by the puking boozers and the French-cropped cunts of England. Whacked off their heads on customised national health prescription anti-depressants. And testosterone injections. And Turkey Twizzlers. They puke up in the lobbies of banks. They use their bank cards to go and puke in a bit of peace and quiet. Leave it there. Welcome to Barclays!

And the girls are so vapid. You know the type? All brown skin and puppy fat and distressed denim on their arses and ponchos.

He continues to work.

When Jade's gone I think I'm going to start spending my time in the bars of Borough Market. Or Sloane Street. Or Bloomsbury. Get myself a rich girl, a business girl. You see them. And below their suits and their handbags and their fresh, fresh skin and clean hair, you know, you just fucking know.

Royalty are the worst, of course. Mind you, if I was the king of this country I'd start every morning with a blowjob too. From my butler. With my coffee and my yoghurt and my fruit. It's the most civilised thing I can imagine. It's absolutely legendary.

Wait here.

He leaves. **Danny** *drinks his water.* **Jade** *shifts her position. He looks at her.*

Danny   Will he be long?

Jade   I don't know.

Pause.

Danny   Doesn't he do your head in after a while?

Jade   What do you mean?

Danny   He goes on a bit, doesn't he?

Jade   I like him.

Danny   Is he your boyfriend?

Jade   Ha!

Danny   What's funny?

Jade   'Is he your boyfriend?'

Danny   What's funny about that?

Jade   Nothing. It doesn't matter.

Danny   You shouldn't laugh at people. Shouldn't laugh at me, definitely. Shouldn't you be at school?

Jade   I don't go to school any more.

Danny   Why not?

Jade   It's boring. I don't need to, anyway. Paul teaches me all kinds of stuff.

Danny   I can imagine.

I used to go Eastbrook. In Dagenham. You ever heard of it?

Jade   No.

Danny   It's a fucking remarkable place. For a thousand reasons. But I never really felt completely comfortable there, you with me?

Jade   –

Danny   I always wanted to go out. See, you'd get a day like this. Go down the docks. Fuck that lot. Go and watch the river. Go over the Chase. Don't you think, Jade?

Jade   –

Danny   Have a day trip. We should have a day trip. Us two. Me and you, Jade. What do you think?

Jade   I don't think Paul would like it.

Danny   He wouldn't mind. Would he?

Paul *comes back in with the gun complete.*

Danny   Would you Paul? Would you mind if I took Jade for a day trip? Hop in the car. Go to the seaside.

Paul *looks at him for a long time. Hands him back his gun.*

Paul   Do you need ammunition?

Danny   I do, yeah.

Paul   Here. 125 gram, nine-millimetre standard pressure hollow-point. Fifty rounds, ten pounds. Sixty pounds total. That's a very good price.

Danny   Thank you.

Paul *hands him a small, plain, red box.* **Danny** *hands him sixty pounds. He examines his gun with a confidence and proficiency that belies the notion that he is anything other than a soldier.*

Paul   This weather.

Danny   Yeah.

Paul   This whole planet is in a terrible state, Danny, you know? The ecological fallout of the decisions that you have made – you, Danny, personally, today, you, not anybody else, you – the ecological fallout of those decisions is catastrophic. And it's the same for all of us. Times sixty million. Times six billion. And nobody says anything about it. There are too many people. There is not enough water. There is not enough oxygen. And nobody admits it. And so now we're gonna consume China. And then we're gonna consume India and then we're gonna consume Africa and we'll carry on consuming. We'll continue to eat it all up and eat it all up and eat it all up until the only thing we've got left to fucking eat, Danny, the only thing we've got left to eat is each other.

Scene Five

Danny *and* **Marley**.

Danny   We could get a car. Get a nice one. CD player. Seat belts. Airbags. All that. A really silent one. Get a couple of kids. Drive them to school. Nip off to work in yer suit. See you later, Danny. See you later, Lee! Have a good day, boys. Do all that.

Marley   Danny.

Danny   Are you cold?

Marley   What are you doing here?

Danny   I got something for yer.

Marley   You can't come round here any more.

Danny   You could make us all a cup of tea in the morning. We could buy a fucking Teasmade! You'd be in for Danny and Lee when they got home from school. I'd be at work but get home later and watch the news!

Marley   This is stupid.

Danny   Do you remember my flat?

Marley

Danny   It was good there, wasn't it? I wish I never sold it. I've nowhere to go now.

Marley   Danny, you're shaking. I'm gonna call your brother.

Danny   I'll tell you something. The amount of fucking snatch I'm gonna get now, Marley, you wouldn't believe.

Marley   The amount of what?

Danny   I already met somebody. We're going on a date. Jade, she's called. Black girl. A fucking coon. How d'yer like that?

Marley   Don't, Danny.

Danny Don't what?

Marley It's boring.

Danny You know how old she is?

Marley –

Danny Have a guess.

Marley No.

Danny She's forty-three.

Marley Great.

Danny That's the level I'm pitching it at nowadays.

Marley Lovely.

Danny Did you see me on the telly, by the way?

Marley I didn't, no.

Danny I was fucking brilliant. Made fucking Paxo look like . . .

Marley That's not what I heard.

Danny You what?

Marley I heard you could barely speak. Didn't look anything like you. You look terrible, Danny. What have you been doing?

Danny I've been at my folks, all day, really.

Marley How they doing?

Danny They're doing all right. They're well. I mean, I hate them so it's difficult for me to tell.

Marley You hate them?

Danny I do a bit. My dad mainly. Drunken fucking contradictory wanker. I find him completely ridiculous. I hope I get to bury him.

She looks at him for a long time.

What are you thinking?

Marley   Are you gonna go up London soon? And look at things?

Danny   What do you mean?

Marley   All the tourist attractions. You used to go, do you remember? Stand outside them. Looking in.

Pause. He glares at her. Then grins.

Danny   When I've finished with you I'm going to go and find every boyfriend you ever had and every friend you ever had and get them and shoot them in the face.

Marley   You what?

Danny   And all your family.

Marley   That's nice, Danny.

Danny   Do you think I won't, Marley, do you think I wouldn't? This is what I'm trained to do.

Marley   I think you need to go to the hospital.

Danny   I've got something for you. I went out, into town, up London, this afternoon and got a present for you. I've not decided whether you're gonna get it yet.

Marley   A present?

Danny   I don't know if you'll like it or not. You probably won't.

Marley   What are you like, Danny? Jesus!

Danny   You look quite sexy when you get angry.

Marley   I'm going now.

Danny   What about your present?

Marley   I don't want your poxy present. What is it? Box of chocolates, is it? Box of Black Magic?

You should know. I wanted to tell you. I do have a boyfriend. I've been seeing him for years. We're gonna get married, I think. We're gonna have kids. I'm gonna be a mum to his kids.

He can't look at her.

All you ever do is talk and talk and talk.

I can't do this any more. It does me no good.

Danny   –

Marley   You're shivering.

Danny   I'm sorry.

Marley   What are you sorry for?

Danny   It's not me. It isn't me.

Marley   What isn't you? Fucking hell!

Danny   I'm really sorry.

Marley   I wanted to be your mate. I wanted to come round for tea and fags and biscuits.

Danny   I don't think so. Not now. No.

Marley.

Marley   What?

Danny   Marley.

Marley   Are you crying?

Danny   Marley.

Marley   What, Danny? Jesus!

Danny   Go back in. You should go back inside. I don't think I should see you any more.

Scene Six

Danny *and* **Jade**.

Danny   It's lovely here, isn't it?

Jade   –

Danny   Most people don't even know this place exists. Some maps don't even show the road onto it.

See his face, on the checkpoint, when I showed him my pass. That was a bit of a surprise for him, I think. What do you think?

Jade   I don't know.

Danny   Sorry?

Jade   I said I don't know.

Danny   It was, I think. I think it was a big surprise. Uptight cunt. Officer class. Failed.

Jade   What are you gonna do?

Danny   See miles from here and all, can't you? See France, I reckon, on a good day.

Jade   Are you gonna hurt me?

Danny   Or Holland. What do you think, Jade? Do you reckon you could see Holland from here?

Jade   I don't know.

Danny   Do you think he'll notice you've gone – Paul?

Jade   Yeah.

Danny   Do you?

Jade   Yes, I do.

Danny   Do you think you were very important to him?

Jade   Yes.

Danny   Do you think he was a bit in love with you, Jade?

Jade   I don't know.

Danny   You looked very funny when I turned up. Did you get the fright of your life?

Jade   I did a bit.

Danny   Did you?

Jade   Yeah.

Danny (*as though to a cute puppy*)   Aaahhh.

A pause. He moves away from her. Looks out to sea.

Were you good at school?

Jade   What?

Danny   When you went to school, Jade, were you quite good at it?

Jade   Yeah.

Danny   I bet you were. You look as though you were. You're quite confident, aren't you? Did you *ever* like it?

Jade   Yeah.

Danny   When did you enjoy it?

Jade   In primary school. Year seven was all right.

Danny   And then it all went a bit wrong for you?

Jade   –

Danny   Would you ever go back, do you think? Go sixth form?

Jade   I think so, yeah.

Danny   'Cause you're quite brainy, aren't you? For your age?

Jade   I don't know.

Danny   What would you do if you did?

Jade   I'm not sure.

Danny   What A levels would you take?

Jade   I –

She starts crying a bit.

Danny   Well, that's clever. You're gonna stay on at sixth form but you don't know what you're going to study there.

Jade   I haven't decided.

Danny   See, that's the fucking thing, isn't it? Nowadays. Young people today! They have no idea what they're going to fucking *do* with their lives. They have no clarity. No vision. No perspective. I find it very dispiriting I have to say.

Stop crying.

I hate students.

Jade   Do you?

Danny   I *fucking* hate sixth-formers. All fucking iPods and crappy T-shirts with band names on.

Do you like the sea, Jade, do yer?

Jade   Yeah.

Danny   Have you ever been out past Southend before?

Jade   No.

Danny   Foulness Island. What a funny name! How old are you Jade?

Jade   I'm sixteen.

Danny   That's not what Paul told me. He told me you were fourteen. Are you fourteen or sixteen?

Jade   Sixteen

Danny   Are you lying to try to impress me?

Jade   No.

Danny   Have you ever actually had sex before?

Jade   What?

Danny   You could look all right, you, you know? If you sorted yourself out a bit, I think you could. Sort your hair out. Your hair looks shit. There could be something of the Britney Spears about you. Do you like her? Britney? Do you, Jade? Stop crying. Jade, do you like Britney Spears?

Will you sing one of her songs for me? Jade? Have you got a good singing voice? Come on, Jade. Sing that, do you know that, that one with the school uniform on, that one 'Baby One More Time'?

Do you know that one, Jade?

Come on. You know it. Britney Spears, Jade.

He sings the first line of the song, encouraging her to sing along with him. He does a little dance while he's singing.

He forgets the words, hums them. Can't stop himself laughing while he's singing.

He remembers the chorus. Sings it. At his manic encouragement she begins to join in.

He stops singing before the final line of the chorus. Waits for her to finish the line. Leans right in on her. Big grin on his face. She sings the final line of the chorus alone.

He nearly hits her. Hard. On the side of her head. Stops his fist just in time. Bursts out laughing.

Danny   Do you want to travel, Jade, do you think?

Jade   What are you going to do to me, please?

Danny   Where do you want to go? Tell me somewhere. Tell me where you wanna go. Tell me some places.

Jade   –

Danny   Do you want to do a geography quiz?

Jade   –

Danny   Capital cities! Ask me a capital cities question, Jade.
Go on. Ask me, 'What's the capital of . . . ?', Jade. You ask me.
'What's the capital of . . . ?' Go on, Jade.

Jade   I don't know.

Danny   You say, 'What's the capital of . . . ?' Say that, Jade!
Say it! Please!

Jade   What's the capital of . . . ?

Danny   And then you think of a country. Say it again, Jade,
and think of a country.

Jade   What's the capital of . . . ?

Danny   Go on, Jade.

Jade   Bulgaria?

Danny   Sofia! See! Sofia! How fucking brilliant is that?!
How many men could do that, Jade?! Not fucking many, that's
how many! Not. Fucking. Many!

Do you know how many words I can spell? Do you? Jade?
Thousands of words. I can spell thousands of words, Jade.
More than anybody I know.

Do you know how many press-ups I can do? Jade, look at me.
I can do a hundred press-ups.

Here. Feel my muscles, Jade. Feel them.

He flexes his bicep. She refuses to move her arm to touch it.

FEEL MY MUSCLES, JADE!

She does.

They're hard, aren't they? Aren't my muscles hard, Jade?

Jade   Yes.

Danny   I know. Here. Watch this!

*He falls to the floor and does ten one-armed press-ups. Counts them all
as he does them.*

Isn't that great?! Not many people can do that, Jade. Not many
people can.

She barely dares look at him.

I like your jacket.

Jade   Thank you.

Danny   Is it new?

Jade   No.

Danny   It looks it.

Jade   It isn't.

Danny   It looks all shiny. Clothes are funny when they feel all new, aren't they? When they smell new. It's a good feeling, that, I think.

Take it off.

Jade   What?

Danny   I wanna take a photograph of you. On my phone.

Would you mind if I took a photograph of you, Jade? Here. Take your, your, take your jacket off, will ya? That's better. There. That's lovely. Gissa smile. Lovely.

He pulls a mobile phone out of his pocket and takes a photograph of her.

Do you want a Coca Cola? Do you? You want some Coke? I've got some Coca Cola in the car. Or how about a smoothie? Do you want a yoghurt and honey smoothie? I love yoghurt and honey smoothies, me.

Put your hand down. On the ground.

Jade   –

Danny   Put it there.

Jade   Don't.

Danny   Jade. Now.

She puts one hand on the ground. He takes another photograph.

Now keep it there.

Jade   –

Danny   I'm going to go and get some Coca Cola and a yoghurt and honey smoothie from the car. I'm not going to tell you when I'm coming back. But when I come back I want your hand to be there.

Jade   Please don't.

He smiles at her briefly, then leaves. She keeps her hand on the ground.

He comes back in with a bottle of Coca Cola, a small honey and yoghurt smoothie, a canister of petrol, a body-bag folded up, a cushion and a cigarette in his mouth.

He lights the cigarette. He smokes it for a while, watching her. He puts the cigarette out on her hand. She screams. Starts crying.

Danny   Did I say that you could move your hand?

Jade   No.

Danny   No, I didn't. I didn't tell you you could move your hand. So why – Jade, Jade, look at me – why did you move your hand, Jade?

Jade   Because you burnt me.

Danny *bursts into a giggle. Then stops. Gathers himself. Takes another photograph with his phone. Looks at her for a while.*

Danny   Sometimes there are days when my heart fills up.

Here. Take your shoes off. Take your socks off.

We had. There was. Our sergeant-major. He was a funny man. I quite liked him, as it goes. You hear all these stories, don't you? Attention! But, no, he was all right. He'd get drunk. Do this to you.

He hits the soles of her feet with the butt of his gun.

With a hammer. Never did it to me. Hurts, doesn't it? And when he shouts at you. SIT FUCKING STILL, JADE! The feeling of spittle on yer face. Here. I'll wipe it off.

He wipes her face.

And you can't tell anybody. You can't pull rank. You can't do that. Get a bucket of shit and piss from the slops of the drains there. Get some little geek cunt. Pour it over their head. It was quite funny. And out there. Everybody says about the British. How fucking noble we are. I used to like the Yanks. At least they were honest about it. At least they had a sense of humour. Yer get me?

He imitates the famous Lynndie England 'Thumbs up!' sign right in her face. And takes an American accent.

Thumbs up, Mac!

Some of the things we did, down in Basra. It was a laugh. I'll tell yer that for nothing. Here, Ali Baba. Get that down yer throat, yer raghead cunt.

You never know. Fucking fourteen-year-old girl? Don't matter. Could've strapped herself. Underneath her fucking burka. Take it off!

Jade   What?

Danny   Take it off! Take you're burka off, this is a body search. I've seen boys with their faces blown off. Skin all pussed up and melted. Eyeballs hanging out on the cartilage.

Yer helmet holds it all together. Bits of yer skull held in.

Will you pretend you're my sister? Jade?

Jade   –

Danny   Will you, Jade?

Jade   If you want.

Danny   Thanks.

Takes another photograph with his phone.

Jade   It's muscle.

Danny   What?

Jade   It's muscle, not cartilage – that holds the eyeball into the skull.

He looks at her for a bit.

Danny   Yeah.

Looks at her for a bit more.

Course you come back. Go up London. Fucking burkas all over the place.

He picks up the petrol canister.

Now here's a question for you. Is this really petrol or is it water?

He opens the canister. Holds it open, under her nose, for her to sniff.

What do you think? Jade? What do you think? Answer me.

Jade   I don't know.

Danny   No, I know. But have a guess. What do you reckon?

Jade   I think it's petrol.

Danny   Do yer?

Jade   It smells like petrol.

Danny   Are you sure that's not just your imagination?

Jade   No. I don't know.

Danny   Your imagination plays terrible fucking tricks on you in situations like this.

He pours some over her head.

You look quite funny. Your hair's all wet.

Takes another photograph with his phone.

You want a cigarette?

He pulls a cigarette out of his packet. Offers it to her. She doesn't take it. He pops it in his mouth. Crouches down. Pulls out a box of matches.

Jade   No.

Danny   Should we?

Jade   No, please, no, don't, don't, don't, don't. Please.

Danny   Chicken. Coward.

He pulls out his gun and presses it into the cushion against her chest. He shoots her in the chest four times. There is no scream. Not much blood is apparent at first. Just four dull thuds. She slumps over a bit. He takes another photograph with his phone.

He drags her body towards the body-bag, leaving a massive trail of blood behind her. The shots have blown her back off. Puts her into the body-bag. Zips it up. He talks to her while he's working.

Yer see them, don't yer?

Fucking leave university and get a fucking house together and spend all day in their shitehawk little jobs hoping that one day they're gonna make it as a fucking big shot. But they're not. They never will. They're shrivelled up home counties kids and they march against the war and think they're being radical. They're lying. They're monkeys. They're French exchange students. They're Australians in London wrecked on cheap wine and shite beer. They're Hasidic Jews in swimming pools. They're lesbian cripples with bus passes. They're niggers, with their faces all full of their mama's jerk chicken, shooting each other in the back down Brixton high street until the lot of them have disappeared. They're little dickless Paki boys training to be doctors or to run corner shops and smuggling explosives in rucksacks onto the top decks of buses. It's not funny, Jade. I'm not joking. I fought a war for this lot.

I want to get it right. That isn't the right word. What's the right word? I want to get the right word. Don't tell me. Don't tell me. Don't tell me. I want to get it right.

I need a massage.

I can't even see straight.

Have I got a stammer? Have you noticed that?

Scene Seven

Danny *and* **Justin** *and* **Helen**.

Danny   Do you know any good dentists?

Justin   I'm sorry?

Danny   I was just wondering if you knew any good dentists. I've got the most fucking horrible toothache.

Justin   Not round here.

Helen   We're not actually from round here.

Justin   I've a good dentist in Chalk Farm, but that's no use.

Danny   No.

Justin   I'm sorry.

Danny   That's okay.

Helen   Toothache's dreadful.

Danny   Yeah. I fucking hate the dentist and all. It's terrifying. The sound of the drill and that.

Is that where you live? Chalk Farm?

Helen   It is, yes.

Danny   Whereabouts?

Helen   Do you know Chalk Farm?

Danny   A little, yeah.

Helen   Fitzjohn's Avenue. Just west of Rosslyn Hill. Do you know that bit?

Danny   No. I don't. I've no idea.

Helen   It's lovely.

Danny   Is it very expensive?

Helen   It is, yes.

Danny   Great!

Helen   I'm Helen.

Danny   Hi, Helen. I'm Danny.

Helen   Hello, Danny. How lovely to meet you.

Danny   And you, yeah.

Justin   I'm Justin.

Danny   Nice one. Arright, Justin?

Justin   Hello mate.

Danny   What brings you down here then?

Justin   We often come to The Northview.

Danny   Oh yeah?

Justin   It's our favourite hotel.

Danny   Right.

Helen   For a day out. A night off. A night out.

Danny   Great.

Helen   We just get in the car. Book a room. Spend the night.

Danny   Lovely.

Helen   I love the sea.

Danny   Yeah, me too.

Helen   The pier. And the funfair.

Danny   Do yer?

Helen   It's marvellous.

Danny   That's funny to me, that.

Helen   Why?

Danny   You just don't strike me as the funfair type.

Helen   Don't I?

Danny   No.

Justin   Doesn't she?

Danny   No.

Helen   Well, I am.

Justin   She is.

Helen   What kind of type do I strike you as, Danny?

Danny   I have no fucking idea.

Justin   Whereabouts are you from Danny?

Danny   I'm from Dagenham.

Justin   Marvellous.

Danny   In Essex.

Justin   Yes. I know it. Up the A13.

Danny   That's right.

Justin   The Ford Factory.

Danny   Uh-huh.

Justin   The World of Leather!

Danny   I'm sorry?

Justin   There's a massive World of Leather in Dagenham. You can get leather sofas there.

Danny   I never knew that.

Justin   It's a marvellous place. Would you like a drink?

Danny   I'm – I don't know.

Justin   We're having a drink.

Helen   Join us.

Justin   Come on, mate, join us for a drink.

Danny   I don't know if I should. I'm driving. I've got a delivery in the boot. I've not eaten – it'd go right to my head.

Justin   We're just about to eat ourselves.

Helen   Yes. Would you like something to eat?

Danny   I don't have –

Helen   Maybe we could buy you a meal or something?

Danny   Thank you. I'll – I'll have a beer with you.

Helen   We'll see about the meal.

Danny   Yeah.

Justin   Yes.

Helen   Good. Lovely.

Justin   What are you delivering?

Danny   I'm sorry?

Justin   In your boot, what is it that you're delivering?

Danny   Fireworks.

Justin   Fireworks?!

Helen   How exciting!

Danny   Is it?

Justin   Why on earth have you got a delivery of fireworks in the boot of your car?

Danny   I arrange firework displays.

Justin   Do you?

Danny   You know, for football matches. Things like that.

Helen   Terrific.

Danny   When West Ham got promoted. I did that.

Helen   Isn't that marvellous?

Justin   Trevor Brooking!

Danny   Yeah.

Justin   What beer would you like?

Danny Er . . .

Justin They have a fantastic selection of multinational lagers.

Danny A lager's fine. A pint of lager would be smashing. Thanks, Justin.

Justin *leaves.* **Helen** *crosses her legs. Stares at* **Danny**. **Danny** *feels his tooth. A time.*

Helen You're rather gorgeous, aren't you?

Danny I'm sorry?

Helen Don't apologise. (*Beat.*) Do you work out?

Danny Do I? No. No. No, I don't.

Helen You've got very broad shoulders.

Danny I used to be a soldier.

Helen Did you?

Danny Until a year or so ago.

Helen I see.

Danny I was out in Basra, as it goes. When that all kicked off.

Helen Good God.

Danny Yeah.

Helen That must have been awful.

Danny No. No. No. No. It was all right. It was fine.

Helen Are you married, Danny?

Danny I am, yeah.

Helen What's your wife called?

Danny Marley.

Helen What a lovely name! How long have you been married to Marley, Danny?

Danny   Ten years. We were at school together. We got married just after we left sixth form.

Helen   How lovely.

Danny   Yeah.

Helen   Where's Marley now?

Danny   She's at home.

Helen   Is she expecting you back?

Danny   She is, yeah.

Helen   I see.

Justin *returns with a pint of lager.*

Danny   Thanks, Justin.

Justin   That's my pleasure.

Danny   You not having one?

Justin   No, no. We're all right.

Helen   We're fine.

A pause. **Danny** *drinks a big gulp of lager.*

Helen   A hard day?

Danny   Yeah. It was a bit, as it goes.

That tastes lovely.

What do you do, Justin?

Justin   I'm a schoolteacher.

Danny   Are you?

Justin   I am, yes. Well. I'm the head of year. At a grammar school. In Tottenham.

Danny   I always hated schoolteachers.

Justin   Is that right?

Danny   Well. I say that. It's actually a lie. They always used to hate me. I would often hanker after their affections. Never got it. It was a big disappointment to me.

Justin   I can imagine.

Danny   Do you work?

Helen   I do, yes.

Danny   What do you do?

Helen   I manage a television production company.

Danny   That sounds pretty, er, exhausting.

Helen   It is.

Danny   Does it affect you at all?

Helen   How do you mean?

Danny   My dad was in management. It gave him a certain demeanour. I think it affected his posture a bit. He used to stand up incredibly straight.

Helen   I'm not sure. I've never thought about it. You have a look. Let me know.

She stands to leave. Speaks to **Justin** *first.*

Helen   I think so, don't you?

Justin *smiles. The two men watch her leave.* **Danny** *drinks.*

Some time passes.

Danny   Thank you for the beer. It's lovely. Really hits the spot.

Justin   That's my pleasure. Honestly.

Pause.

Danny   Yeah.

Some time.

Justin   So. Fireworks.

Danny   That's right.

Some time passses. **Justin** *looks right at him.*

Justin   Helen's my wife.

Danny   I guessed that.

Justin   We've actually got two children.

Danny   Oh, right.

Justin   David is four and Phillipa's two.

Danny   Lovely.

Justin   They're staying with her mother tonight.

Danny   Right.

Justin   Have you been to this hotel before?

Danny   I haven't, no.

Justin   I didn't think you had.

Danny   It's all right, isn't it? The views and that.

Justin   It is. Yes. We're staying in Room 21.

Danny   I'm sorry?

Justin   Room 21.

Some time passes.

Danny *breaks into a big grin.* **Justin** *smiles with him.*

Danny   Fucking hell.

Justin   Don't say anything now.

Some time.

Helen *comes back. They sit together for a bit.* **Justin** *and* **Helen** *exchange glances, slight smiles, while* **Danny** *drinks more of his beer.*

Danny   Justin was just telling me about your children.

Helen   What did he say about them?

Danny   He told me how old they were.

Helen   Did he? Did you?

Justin   I did.

Danny   Four and two, wasn't it? David and Phillipa?

Helen   That's right.

Justin   Pip, I call her.

Helen   He's completely devoted to her. Aren't you?

Justin   I am a bit, I'm afraid.

Helen   He's absolutely under her thumb. She's got him twisted round her little finger.

Danny   He invited me up to your room.

Helen   Did he?

Danny   I'm a bit fucking freaked out, as it goes.

Helen   I thought you would be. There's no need to be.

Danny was telling me, Justin, while you were at the bar. He used to be in the army.

Justin   You can tell that.

Helen   That's what I thought. He was in Basra, apparently.

Justin   Were you really?

Danny *chuckles a bit.*

Justin   Would you like another beer?

Danny   No, thank you. I'm all right.

Justin   It's not a big deal, you know? It's just an invitation. I think Helen finds you quite attractive. But you mustn't do anything that you don't want to do.

Danny   No. No. No. It's not that. It's just a surprise.

Helen   It's just sex.

Danny   Yeah. I think it's good. My mum never bothered asking my dad. I think it's very open-minded. Does that come with working in the media, do you think?

Helen   I'm not entirely sure.

Danny   And do you like to watch, do you?

Justin   Only if it's not a problem.

Danny   Or do you join in?

Justin   I think that's . . .

Helen   That can be up to you.

Danny   Right.

Helen *stands up.*

Helen   I think you two should decide that. I'll be back.

She leaves.

Danny   I guess it's one of those things, isn't it? That you read about.

Justin   I don't know, is it?

Danny   It goes on all the time, I bet.

Justin *nods.*

Danny   Do you like it? Watching?

Justin   I do, yes.

Danny   Why?

Justin   I think it's lovely. I like to watch her happy.

Danny   Right. That's quite sweet, as it goes.

Justin *smiles.*

Danny   It's not like it's the first time I've ever come across this kind of thing, you know.

Justin   No?

Danny   In our platoon. You could go, sometimes, into downtown Basra.

Justin   Really?

Danny   Or not even bother. You could just stay in the barracks. Fuck each other. That would happen. You can't blame people, can you?

Justin   I never would.

Danny   You do get a little bored after a while.

Justin   I can imagine.

Danny   Smell of a nice bit of aftershave. Nice but of stubble on a chin. All the same with your eyes closed, isn't it? There is a certain attraction, I think.

Justin   I think so, too.

Danny   I thought you would. I was lying. Yer gay cunt.

Justin   I don't believe you.

Danny   You what?

Justin   I don't believe you were lying.

Helen *comes back. There is a time. She stares at him. Grins.*

Helen   You're still here. I'm glad. (*To* **Justin**.) Thank you.

Justin *smiles at* **Danny**.

Danny   Did you go on the march?

Justin   On the –

Danny   On the anti-war march, up Hyde Park, did you two go on that?

Justin   Yes. We did.

Danny *laughs*.

Danny   Did yer?!

Helen   Why's that funny?

Danny   I wish I'd been there.

Justin   Do you?

Danny   With my SA80. Sprayed the lot of yer. Stick that up yer arse and smoke it, Damon Albarn, yer fucking pikey cunt.

Helen and **Justin** *smile at one another.*

Helen   Yes.

Danny   I come back home. It's a completely foreign country.

He reaches over to **Helen**. *Strokes her cheek.*

'Do you work out?' What the fuck are you talking about? Two hours drill and forty lengths. Twenty-five minutes max. Alternate strokes. Breaststroke, front crawl, back-stroke, butterfly.

He puts his thumb in her mouth. She sucks on it.

Here, you'll like this. I saw, one time, a group of guys, at Pirbright, get another lad, a younger lad – no listen to this, this is right up your street. They get him. Hold him down. Get a broom handle. Fucking push it, right up his rectum. Right up there. (*He removes his thumb.*) And we all watched that. Joined in. That was funny, to be fair. It did feel funny. I imagine it's the same kind of feeling, is it?

Helen   Are you trying to unnerve us?

Danny   Mind you, you play that game out there and it's even funnier. 'Cause they don't like anything with the slightest sexual connotation. You two, out there! Fucking hell!

Justin (*smiling*)   I think he is.

Helen   Do you?

Danny   I'd put it on my phone. You wanna see what I've got on my phone? You wanna see Ken Bigley? I've got Ken Bigley on here. Nick Berg. All them! You wanna watch?

Justin   I think you are.

Danny   You wanna watch, Justin?

Justin   No, I don't.

Danny *stares at him.*

Danny   Do you know what I want to do?

Helen   What's that?

Danny   I want an arm-wrestle. Right now. I fucking love arm-wrestles, me. Do you want one, Justin?

Helen   You're rather funny, aren't you?

Justin (*chuckling*)   He's like a little boy.

Danny   Justin. Come here. Let's have an arm-wrestle.

He positions his arm. Glares at him.

Come on, mate.

Justin *braces* **Danny***'s arm in an arm-wrestle.* **Danny** *holds his arm exactly where he wants it.*

Danny   I've put children into the backs of ambulances and they've not *got* any arms, actually.

It could happen here, all that. I reckon it will. There are too many people. Wait until the water runs out. And the oxygen runs out.

Justin   Are you trying your hardest?

Danny   I'm gonna convert to Islam. Save me from scumballs like you two.

I'm not apologising for anything. See me. I'm as innocent as a baby. I'm a fucking hero! I'm a fucking action hero! I'm John fucking Wayne! I'm Sylvester Stallone! I'm fucking James Bond, me!

He wins the arm-wrestle.

That was fucking easy.

Scene Eight

Danny *and* **Lee**.

Lee I spoke to Mum.

Danny Right.

Lee I told them to tell anybody who asks that you were with them all day.

Danny Right.

Lee She said she would. She said that Dad would too. She said it's not a problem. They've not been out. They've not spoken to anybody.

Danny Which is lucky.

Lee Yes. Yes. Yes. Yes. It is. Yes. They won't ask.

Danny What?

Lee Mum and Dad. They won't ask why they've got to lie for you.

Danny No.

Lee They'll just do it. They'll do whatever I ask them to.

Danny Right. Yeah. Course they will. What'll you say?

Lee I, I, I, I, I, I, I, I –

They look at each other for a long time.

Danny I've had one hell of a day.

They look at each other for a long time.

It's horrible round here. They should set it on fire.

They look at each other for a long time.

Don't tell anybody, Lee. Don't you dare. Do you understand me?

Lee Of course I do.

Danny   You fucking better.

Lee   What are you going to do?

Danny   When?

Lee   If the police find you?

Danny   I'll shoot them in the face and then shoot myself in the face and all.

Lee   I'm being serious.

Danny   So am I, Lee.

Pause.

Lee   Can I see it?

Danny   See what?

Lee   Your gun.

Danny *gets his gun out of his pocket and shows it to* **Lee**. **Lee** *holds it with a mix of complete horror and absolute fascination.*

Danny   It's hot, isn't it? We should go out. Take our shoes off. Get the grass between our toes.

So.

Blackburn next week, Lee.

Lee (*completely transfixed by the gun*)   That's right. Mark Hughes was a good player. Sparky, they called him.

Danny   Are you going to go, do you think?

Lee   I don't think so, no.

Danny   Have you ever actually been? To a game?

Lee   No. I haven't, no.

Danny   Why not?

Lee   I don't know. I haven't.

Danny   I wish I had a sister. It would have been miles better.

Lee   How much money have you got, exactly?

Danny   Three thousand, two hundred pounds.

Lee   Right. That's one good thing. (*Beat.*) Where is she, Danny?

Danny   She's in the boot of the car.

Lee   What are you gonna do with her?

Danny   I have no idea.

Lee *gives the gun back.*

Lee   Have my fingerprints all over that now. They'll think I did it.

Danny   Nobody'll notice that she's gone, you know?

Lee   They will. She was fourteen.

Danny   You didn't know her. She wasn't like most fourteen-year-olds.

Lee   This is stupid. You're stupid. You're a stupid stupid stupid stupid stupid –

Danny   What?

I wish it hadn't happened, Lee.

Lee   Do you?

Danny   If that's any consolation.

Lee   It isn't.

Danny   She was like a doll. She was a cute little black thing.

How was your lunch?

Lee   It was very nice, thank you.

Danny   What did you have?

Lee   I had roast pork and apple sauce and roast potatoes and gravy and carrots and peas and cauliflower.

Danny   You wouldn't get that free if you were living with Mum and Dad, would you? Doctors wouldn't come round then, would they?

Lee   I don't think so.

Danny   Is that the main reason you left, Lee, for yer dinners? Do you really think you deserve this place?

Lee   I don't know.

Danny   Is that why you keep it so fucking clean?

Lee   Danny.

Danny   Do you think it's Mum and Dad's fault, what's happening to you? Is it genetic, do you think?

Lee   Don't you start swearing your head off again!

Danny   Did you have a hundred fucking mercury fillings or what?

Lee   Danny.

Danny   You don't have the slightest idea what I'm going through.

Lee   I spend my nights watching reruns of *The Simpsons* on the television. I have videos of *Mork and Mindy* that I watch sometimes. And I spend my days trawling sex-contact pages on the internet. Don't you tell me that I don't know what you're going through. I *live* what you're going through. And I never did anything like that!

Danny   Ha!

Lee   Did you go and see Marley?

Pause.

Danny   I did, yeah.

Lee   I told you not to go.

Danny   I know.

Lee   You liked her, didn't you?

Danny   I did, yeah.

Lee   You liked her a bit too much, I think. You would've married her, I bet.

Danny   Lee.

Lee   She would never have married you, would she though, Danny? You were completely deluding yourself.

I'm so much cleverer than you, in real life, it's embarrassing.

When you were on television. I was incredulous. You couldn't even finish your sentences.

'It's important to think that we're making a difference. People have no idea what life was like here under Saddam's regime.'

Thing is. Mum and Dad were extremely proud of you. They had arguments. Over which one of them you took after and which one I took after.

He's ashamed of me, Dad. Which is ironic. People used to say I was a paedophile. Largely because of my glasses. I think he used to believe them. And if it weren't for you, I would have had a much more horrible time than I actually did. People were frightened you would have battered them. On account of you being a psychopath. I know that. But I can't do this, I don't think.

Danny   Do what?

Lee   Your eyes.

Danny   What can't you do, Lee?

Lee   I'm not surprised that girls like you. You've got nice eyes. They look for nice eyes in a man, I heard.

Danny   Lee, I asked you a question.

Lee   I don't think I can not tell. I think I'm going to tell the police.

Danny   Lee.

Lee   I don't think I can keep it to myself.

Danny   You can, you can, you can, you can, Lee.

Lee   Are you gonna batter my head in now?

Danny   You so can. You so can.

Lee   Why should I?

Danny   You're my brother.

They look at each other for a long time. The longest that they can manage. And then **Danny** *moves away.*

Ah, fuck it! Eh? Eh, Lee? Fuck it! You know?

It doesn't matter.

What does it matter?

Here. Bruv. Come here. I'm sorry I was mean to you! I think you're the best. I think you're fucking gorgeous. Come here.

Lee *approaches him.*

Danny   Touch my chest.

Lee *rests his hand on his chest.*

Danny   There. How hard is that? You like that? Here. Come here.

He beckons **Lee** *towards his face.*

Danny   Come on. Just a kiss. There.

He kisses **Lee**, *on the lips.*

Danny   There. You don't need to tell anybody. Do you?

Have you got a hard on? You have, haven't you? It's all right. It's all right, Lee. Straight up. It's all right. It doesn't matter.

All our years. All of them.

My brother!

He knows what I'm talking about.

When we were kids. Tell yer.

And everybody looks at him like he's some kind of fucked-up fucking weird old cunt. But he's not, yer know.

He's not.

He isn't.

He's all right

He's not gonna tell anybody.

And the way you smell! It's exactly the way I smell too. It reminds me of me. It makes me feel sick.

He kisses **Lee** *hard on the cheek. And breaks away. Lights a cigarette. His hands trembling.*

Lee   You smoke the same brand as Dad's secret cigarettes.

Danny   Right.

Lee   It must be genetic.

Pause.

Danny   Will you cut my hair?

Lee   What?

Danny   I need a haircut.

Lee   All right.

Danny   I've got clippers.

Lee   I don't need your clippers. I've got my own clippers. I'll do it with my clippers. I'll do it great.

He pulls up a chair. **Danny** *sits in it.* **Lee** *wraps a towel round* **Danny**'s *neck. Leaves to go and get his clippers.*

Danny *stares out.*

Lee *comes back after a bit.*

Danny   Shanghai.

Lee   12,762,953.

Danny   Moscow.

Lee   10,381,288.

He stands behind **Danny**, *looks at the back of his head. He has the clippers poised in his hand.*

Danny   In Basra, when it all kicked off with the prisoners, I didn't do any of it. I never touched nobody. I had the rules, pinned above my head. My idiot's guide to the Geneva Convention pinned to the head of my bed. They used to call me a pussy cunt. It never used to bother me. I wish I'd told somebody. I might, still. I wish I'd joined in. I would've liked that.

I don't blame the war.

The war was all right. I miss it.

It's just you come back to this.

Lee   I never touched *any*body.

Danny   You what?

Lee   It's I never touched *any*body. Not I never touched *no*body. That's just careless.

Lee *turns his clippers on. He waits for a while before he starts cutting.*

The lights fall.

Methuen Drama Modern Plays

include work by

Edward Albee
Jean Anouilh
John Arden
Margaretta D'Arcy
Peter Barnes
Sebastian Barry
Brendan Behan
Dermot Bolger
Edward Bond
Bertolt Brecht
Howard Brenton
Anthony Burgess
Simon Burke
Jim Cartwright
Caryl Churchill
Complicite
Noël Coward
Lucinda Coxon
Sarah Daniels
Nick Darke
Nick Dear
Shelagh Delaney
David Edgar
David Eldridge
Dario Fo
Michael Frayn
John Godber
Paul Godfrey
David Greig
John Guare
Peter Handke
David Harrower
Jonathan Harvey
Iain Heggie
Declan Hughes
Terry Johnson
Sarah Kane
Charlotte Keatley
Barrie Keeffe

Howard Korder
Robert Lepage
Doug Lucie
Martin McDonagh
John McGrath
Terrence McNally
David Mamet
Patrick Marber
Arthur Miller
Mtwa, Ngema & Simon
Tom Murphy
Phyllis Nagy
Peter Nichols
Sean O'Brien
Joseph O'Connor
Joe Orton
Louise Page
Joe Penhall
Luigi Pirandello
Stephen Poliakoff
Franca Rame
Mark Ravenhill
Philip Ridley
Reginald Rose
Willy Russell
Jean-Paul Sartre
Sam Shepard
Wole Soyinka
Simon Stephens
Shelagh Stephenson
Peter Straughan
C. P. Taylor
Theatre Workshop
Sue Townsend
Judy Upton
Timberlake Wertenbaker
Roy Williams
Snoo Wilson
Victoria Wood

Methuen Drama World Classics

include

Jean Anouilh (two volumes)
Brendan Behan
Aphra Behn
Bertolt Brecht (eight volumes)
Büchner
Bulgakov
Calderón
Čapek
Anton Chekhov
Noël Coward (eight volumes)
Feydeau
Eduardo De Filippo
Max Frisch
John Galsworthy
Gogol
Gorky (two volumes)
Harley Granville Barker
  (two volumes)
Victor Hugo
Henrik Ibsen (six volumes)
Jarry

Lorca (three volumes)
Marivaux
Mustapha Matura
David Mercer (two volumes)
Arthur Miller (five volumes)
Molière
Musset
Peter Nichols (two volumes)
Joe Orton
A. W. Pinero
Luigi Pirandello
Terence Rattigan
  (two volumes)
W. Somerset Maugham
  (two volumes)
August Strindberg
  (three volumes)
J. M. Synge
Ramón del Valle-Inclán
Frank Wedekind
Oscar Wilde

Methuen Drama Contemporary Dramatists

include

John Arden (two volumes)
Arden & D'Arcy
Peter Barnes (three volumes)
Sebastian Barry
Dermot Bolger
Edward Bond (eight volumes)
Howard Brenton
(two volumes)
Richard Cameron
Jim Cartwright
Caryl Churchill (two volumes)
Sarah Daniels (two volumes)
Nick Darke
David Edgar (three volumes)
David Eldridge
Ben Elton
Dario Fo (two volumes)
Michael Frayn (three volumes)
John Godber (three volumes)
Paul Godfrey
David Greig
John Guare
Lee Hall (two volumes)
Peter Handke
Jonathan Harvey
(two volumes)
Declan Hughes
Terry Johnson (three volumes)
Sarah Kane
Barrie Keefe
Bernard-Marie Koltès
(two volumes)
Franz Xaver Kroetz
David Lan
Bryony Lavery
Deborah Levy
Doug Lucie

David Mamet (four volumes)
Martin McDonagh
Duncan McLean
Anthony Minghella
(two volumes)
Tom Murphy (five volumes)
Phyllis Nagy
Anthony Neilson
Philip Osment
Gary Owen
Louise Page
Stewart Parker (two volumes)
Joe Penhall
Stephen Poliakoff
(three volumes)
David Rabe
Mark Ravenhill
Christina Reid
Philip Ridley
Willy Russell
Eric-Emmanuel Schmitt
Ntozake Shange
Sam Shepard (two volumes)
Wole Soyinka (two volumes)
Simon Stephens
Shelagh Stephenson
David Storey (three volumes)
Sue Townsend
Judy Upton
Michel Vinaver
(two volumes)
Arnold Wesker (two volumes)
Michael Wilcox
Roy Williams (two volumes)
Snoo Wilson (two volumes)
David Wood (two volumes)
Victoria Wood

Lightning Source UK Ltd.
Milton Keynes UK
UKOW06f1802260515

252318UK00009B/555/P